Reviews

"Wow! A hint of C S Lewis, a resemblance to Peter Kreeft and a lot to chew on after reading. Well done. I love your image of God and emphasis on hell as free choice. I've always favoured the theory that Lucifer and his comrades fell when informed that not only was God going to create an animal-spirit hybrid but planned to incarnate as one of them; "Shall I, who am light and flame, worship dust and mud?" The inclusion of war crimes and the idea that all who support a war are implicated in its horrors were powerful."
—John Markson

"You've done an excellent job of researching your topic and it has the ring of truth to it. Your writing flows smoothly and logically. You're aware of where your plot is going and have a sense of what your setting should be for every scene… your script is quite compelling as it keeps us wanting to find out what is to come."
—A friend

"…a thoughtful dissertation and a (literally) fantastic invention that drives home some pretty big truths and challenges some pretty common conventions. It certainly makes the reader think – and have a little fun at the same time."
—Dermot Nolan

"A lot of effort and research is evident. You cover many religious issues through AJ and Bishop Noonan and their foils, Gabriella and Mohammed. When these four characters are interacting the play flows and the information is compelling. It reads very well and is actually a page turner…"
—Robert Fierheller

CRIMES AGAINST CHILDREN

> DISCORD IN THE AFTER-LIFE:
> A BISHOP AND AN ATHEIST
> DENY THEIR CULPABILITY
> FOR ABUSE AND WAR.

Peter Rosser

Copyright © 2019 by Peter Rosser

This book is a work of fiction. Any references to historical events, real people or real places are used fictitiously. Other characters, places and events are products of the author's imagination; and, any resemblance to actual events or locales or persons, living or dead, is entirely coincidental.

Cover design by Emily Shea of Cathedral Student Enterprises.

Dedication

To all the good priests whose ministry has been compromised by the hopeless inaction of their bishops.

Table of Contents

Cast of Characters	xi
1 The Arrivals Hall	1
2 The Passport Control Station	5
3 The Mausoleum	11
4 The Doubters' Morgue	13
5 The Lobby Café, 1st Visit	21
6 The Prayer Room	33
7 The Lobby Café, 2nd Visit	43
8 The Court Room, Bishop Noonan	53
9 The Court Room, AJ	63
10 The Lobby Café, 3rd Visit	71
11 The Holy of Holies	83
12 The Lobby Café, 4th Visit	91
13 The Party	105
Acknowledgments	115
About the Author	117
End Notes	119

"For today Lord let there be more love than hate in this world; more food than weapons."

Cast of Characters

Mohammed:	A middle-eastern man in his 50's
Peter:	A voice only: a member of God's elect
Gabriella:	A woman of colour in her 30's: an archangel
Paul Noonan:	A man in his 80's: a Roman Catholic Bishop
Cemetery Employee:	A woman in her 30's
Funeral Director:	A woman in her 50's
A.J. Forsythe:	A man in his 60's: astrophysicist, author and polemicist
Maggie Forsythe:	A woman in her 50's: first wife of A.J., mother of his children
Theresa de Delores:	A woman in her 30's: child abuse victim
Mariam:	A Muslim mother in her 30's
Omar, Abdullah, and Fatima:	Children of Mariam: Omar (baby); Abdullah, age 3; and Fatima, age 10
God:	A voice only: female, soft yet distinctive
Party Cast:	Men and women from many religious traditions, plus attendants
Doorwoman:	A woman in her 30's
Dimitri:	A big man in his 50's: a Russian Orthodox Bishop
Amanda:	A woman in her 50's: the waitress
Young Woman:	A woman in her 30's: a demon

1
The Arrivals Hall

April 15, 2019. The arrivals hall of a large airport. A multi-coloured neon sign stretching the length of the concourse with letters twelve feet tall continually flashes: **Welcome to the Lobby: the Gateway to Heaven.** *Two large split-flap displays are chattering in the background. The arrivals board lists only names and birthdates of passengers, no flight numbers or cities of origin. Judging from the birthdates, the arriving travelers range from a few days old to over one hundred years. The departures board lists only two destinations: To Be Determined and Express To Heaven. Only children's names are included on the manifest for the Express To Heaven flight.*

Mohammed, wearing a white thobe and red kufi, enters the hall, texting on his phone...looks up and addresses the reader...

Mohammed: Oh, salaam alaikum, I'm *[his phone rings]* excuse me for a moment.
Peter: *[Voice on phone.]* Mohammed?
Mohammed: Peter, salaam alaikum.

Peter: Peace be with you.

Mohammed: How can I help you?

Peter: Mohammed, will you cover an intake for me today?

Mohammed: Certainly, Peter – anyone interesting?

Peter: Roman Catholic Bishop – Paul Noonan.

Mohammed: Ah – cappa magna guy – very stylish I've heard! Does she want me to shake him up a little? Should I look very Muslim? *[Points to his outfit.]*

Peter: Are you trying to read her thoughts again?

Mohammed: Sorry, family trait.

Peter: Sounds like a good idea. I'll have Sandar greet the children. Go in peace Mohammed.

Mohammed: Allahu Akbar. *[Mohammed puts away his phone.]* As I was about to say, welcome to 'The Lobby'. I know, a rather banal name for the gateway to heaven, but it seems to work for all traditions. It's the check-in desk for what's to come, a place for some rather riveting discussions, often quite heated.

[Mohammed returns his focus to his phone. Gabriella enters the hall. She is a tall, young woman of colour, very attractive, with short cut hair. Gabriella is always dressed in an ankle-length flowing dress of a single colour, complemented by a patterned scarf worn around the shoulders or covering the hair, and sandals.]

Gabriella: Mohammed, peace be with you.

Mohammed: Salaam alaikum, Gabriella. *[Gabriella crosses the hall and exits.]* Did you see her? They never age those archangels. I hear that she is also covering intake today – some famous astrophysicist, one of the new atheists. This could be quite the day!

2
The Passport Control Station

The passport control station at the airport. Directly behind the counters is a set of automatic doors with a large sign: **To Be Determined.** *To the right of the counters is another set of doors with an equally large sign:* **Express To Heaven.** *Sign on the front of the counters:* **Please wait behind the yellow line until called.**

Mohammed takes a position at the one of the counters and opens a large ledger. A group of twenty-five children led by a Buddhist nun enters the hall and proceeds directly to the Express To Heaven doors and passes through. Bishop Noonan enters the hall dressed in a black cassock with fuchsia piping, shoulder cape, fuchsia sash and fuchsia zucchetto and prominent pectoral cross. He is alone. He looks around, trying to reconcile what he's seeing with what he has imagined. He reads all the signs and heads towards the Express To Heaven doors.

Mohammed: Paul Noonan? Paul Noonan? *[Bishop Noonan looks towards Mohammed who waves him over.]*

Bishop Noonan: Yes? *[Re-reads the signs and then carefully crosses the yellow line to approach the counter.]* I'm confused. I think I'm in the wrong place. This must be a dream. I'm not sure that I'm dead yet – this is not what it should look like. *[Looking around feverishly, getting himself worked up.]* This seems all wrong! You're a Muslim! I just saw a Buddhist nun – she was with a group of children.

Mohammed: *[Interrupting.]* Oh yes, the school shooting.

Bishop Noonan: Another one…oh, that's terrible… *[lost for words]*…I was expecting to meet Jesus or one of the saints…not this.

Mohammed: Calmly Bishop…take a deep breath. It's quite common to be confused in the beginning. Remember your Vatican II: there are many pathways to God. And, don't worry, we accept Christians.

Bishop Noonan: *[Calmer, but still confused.]* Why does it look like passport control? Why aren't there more people? Where did the nun and the children go? Are you sure I'm in the right place?

[Mohammed holds up his hands in a stop pose and then smiles.]

Mohammed: Allow me to answer in reverse order: yes, you are in the proper place; Sandar – the nun – and the children went through the express entrance, where all the children go; there aren't more people because we have many points of access; and, it looks like passport control because we adapt our intake procedures to reflect the experiences of our guests. Take a good look around, you'll see this closely resembles Fiumicino Airport in Rome. Just for you, Excellency!

Bishop Noonan: *[Still confused.]* Oh, yes, I see... *[pointing to the sign]*...but the sign: *To Be Determined* surely that doesn't apply to me? I know maybe I'm not deserving of the express line, but at least I should qualify for purgatory...I can understand that I require some time for the purification of my soul, I know that my life hasn't been sinless; but, there can't be any possibility of the...the other place. Jesus, Mary and Joseph, are you telling me that purgatory isn't true either?

Mohammed: There is a state that resembles purgatory, but that comes after your final destination has been determined.

Bishop Noonan: You mean there's some doubt? For me?

Mohammed: Of course! For adults, everyone gets to choose – heaven or hell.

Bishop Noonan: *[Processing this idea.]* I understand that God doesn't send people to hell – that it's a free choice to deprive ourselves of his presence...but surely we make that choice through our lives on earth. Now, it's too late. Our decision has been made.

Mohammed: Well not exactly. For most people the choice they made on earth will be the one they make even when they stand in God's presence. But, there are exceptions. God provides a final opportunity for each to choose goodness over evil. Eternity is a very long time.

Bishop Noonan: *[A bit astonished.]* You mean even now there is a chance for reconciliation? That doesn't seem fair!

Mohammed: Not fair – a child's expression. Just and merciful would be better descriptors.

Bishop Noonan: *[Processing this idea.]* And, you're telling me that even with this last minute reprieve and knowing that God actually exists, some people still choose hell? Why?

Mohammed: Pride. Some people cannot acknowledge that they have ever been wrong – especially about the existence of God. That failure was obviously her fault. Some cannot bring…

Bishop Noonan: *[Interrupts.]* Did you say her? *[Mohammed gives two thumbs up.]* Oh, I've got a very bad feeling about this!

Mohammed: *[Continuing.]* Now, where was I? Oh yes… some cannot bring themselves to publicly say that God was there all the time. They would rather delude themselves that their whole existence has been and continues to be a dream. Some people can never forgive or be forgiven. Some wear their hurts like badges of honour and wish to hold these injustices over their transgressors for eternity. Some say they want to be with friends or family members. Some are simply nasty beings.

Bishop Noonan: But surely God would save those that are confused or troubled.

Mohammed: Ah, Bishop – remember your Augustine: "God won't save you without your consent." And some people simply will not consent. The number one rule here is that people rarely change – the way they were on earth is the way they will be here. Even in the presence of the Almighty, last chance conversion is a rare experience.

Bishop Noonan: Can you tell me then what to expect? What's the process? How long will it take? Why are you here?

Mohammed: Paul, may I call you Paul? *[Bishop Noonan nods.]* Paul, I've been assigned to be your guide, to answer your queries as they arise. As to the process: your first task will be to prepare for a rigorous examination of conscience where you will meet many people from your life on earth – people you have harmed, treated badly, ridiculed, dismissed; those for whom you returned disdain for love; anyone you failed to love as you loved yourself. You will then have a chance to redress these wrongs. How long? As long as it takes. In earth time, days at least, perhaps a month or two. *[Bishop Noonan is shaking.]* Enough for now – look, you're shaking. Let's go have a coffee while you reflect on what I've told you thus far.

[Mohammed and Bishop Noonan exit together through the To Be Determined doors. Mohammed has an arm around the Bishop's shoulder. The Bishop's head is slumped.]

3
The Mausoleum

*Inside an ornate mausoleum at the **Pathway to Oblivion Cemetery**, one wall crypt is open. The marble cover for the crypt is prominently displayed on an easel. The cover is inscribed:*

Dr. A.J. Forsythe
Brilliant Astrophysicist
1955-2019
A Man Without Equal

A solitary Cemetery Employee stands adjacent to the crypt. A single Funeral Director enters the mausoleum, pushing an elaborate casket on a trolley.

Cemetery Employee: *[Looks around.]* That's it? No pall bearers; no mourners?

Funeral Director: Very private affair. But if you ask me, it wasn't so much a wish, but the result of a life poorly lived – arrogant asshole apparently. Brilliant but arrogant! Even his kids didn't like him; nor any of the wives, especially the last one. Had the big one in one of his grad student's bed. Besides, the whole lot of them are confirmed atheists. He's gone, time to move on. Colleagues are already fighting over his office space at the university. *[Chuckling.]* You should see the clothes they brought to bury him in!

Cemetery Employee: Unusual though – that group prefers cremation and some form of symbolic scattering. With his money he could have been shot into space and spread around the Hubble Telescope.

Funeral Director: He was, shall we say, a little tight with the dollars and didn't feel right about burning up his fancy coffin. Wanted to get his money's worth.

[Funeral Director and Cemetery Employee slide the casket into the crypt. The two attendants look at the opening one last time; the Funeral Director blesses herself. They nod to each other, and exit the mausoleum together.]

4
The Doubters' Morgue

*The sign over the door reads **Doubters' Morgue**. The room is a square, thirty feet by thirty feet, painted entirely in a light grey. It feels cold. The room is empty save for a solitary coffin resting on a concrete plinth. It is A.J. Forsythe's casket.*

Gabriella enters the room. She approaches the head of the casket and knocks.

Gabriella: Hello, hey in there…

AJ: Yes, hello… Who's there? What? Oh, I'm having a dream.

Gabriella: Focus Dr. Forsythe, focus…it will come back to you. Does your dream involve chest pain and something heavy?

AJ: How did you know? I was in bed with Jessica and then this pain in my chest, like a damn truck was sitting on it; and then…oh, this is a dream. I'm still alive and resting and there's no pain…and no feeling...and, oh shit, does my wife know about Jessica? Or, or...

Gabriella: OK, Dr. Forsythe, do you mind if I call you AJ? *[No reply.]* So, AJ, let's look at 'or'!

AJ: Or...shit. I can feel satin everywhere. I can't move; it's dark and ah...this isn't how it's supposed to be.

Gabriella: How's it supposed to be, AJ?

AJ: Nothing! It's supposed to be nothing! And who are you? And, how do you know my name is AJ?

Gabriella: *[Ignores the questions.]* Well, perhaps you were wrong. Or, maybe you chose wrong; calculated wrong?

AJ: OK, I was wrong! Now, get me out of here! Now!

Gabriella: Well, it doesn't quite work that way.

AJ: What? I'm buried alive? It's OK to leave me here? Don't you understand how horrific this is?

Gabriella: Actually, you are not buried alive. To be precise, you've been encrypted; not buried at all. As to being alive, maybe we should say you're in transition. *[Pausing.]* Sorry, that's a little tangential. Are you in any pain? I expect if you take a true assessment of your state, you feel no physical discomfort. You may feel alone; empty might be the best way to describe it.

AJ: Yes, yes something like that. There's a great nothingness about this. *[Thinking that this might be a permanent state, AJ panics.]* Oh, this would be hell –

alone in the dark. Simply being. Even pain would be better than this.

Gabriella: Ah, there you go, isn't that what you predicted; expected? Nothing. Well, your nothingness has arrived and you are completely capable of experiencing it.

AJ: No. No. There was to be nothing. I wasn't supposed to experience nothing. This is a monumental difference.

Gabriella: Well then, you're having a new experience as we speak. You should take the time to explore this new level of consciousness, while I get someone to look into your situation and expedite your processing.

AJ: *[Now absolutely enraged.]* Processing? Did you say processing? What the hell does that mean? And who are you? And what kind of God leaves people buried alive and suffering? *[Prolonged pause, while Gabriella stares at the ceiling.]* Hey, are you still there? *[Now contritely.]* Please tell me that you're still there. *[Pause.]* Please… *[pause]*… please.

Gabriella: Yes, I'm still here!

AJ: Well, don't you have something to say?

Gabriella: I'm thinking about your comment about the 'kind of God'. I'm a little confused as to how God got into your equation. You don't believe in God. Did you not spend a great deal of your adult life making fun of believers and relishing in having debates with people of faith and mocking their arguments and positions? And I'm sure that you wrote one of those books: *God is Dead, or an Illusion, Delusion; God is Rotten; Faith is Dead*. Oh, I remember you wrote the poetic one: *God is a Fraud*. Awful title! And now, your situation is somehow God's fault? Perhaps you've been right all along and there is no God. Maybe there is consciousness after physical death. Examine the possibilities! Perhaps your string theory has another dimension – a metaphysical space where all consciousness attends. Maybe you are destined for that realm. Or, perhaps your consciousness simply lives for a period of physical time after the death of the body and you will experience another death – sooner or later. Maybe the whole thing is a dream and I'm just a figment of your imagination.

AJ: This is not helpful.

Gabriella: Perhaps there is a God. But then that poses the question: what kind of God is he or she? Perhaps Deus absconditis or Deus otiosis – they have nice rings to them…don't you think? Although neither of those theological constructs is particularly helpful for your situation. Having created you – somewhat indirectly keeping in mind the evolutionary processes – perhaps God got bored and really isn't involved any longer. Creation simply goes on without any God-like interventions.

AJ: So…

Gabriella: So… You could be stuck there until he or she shows some renewed interest. Of course, the question would then have to be asked, "Why should he or she have any renewed interest in you in particular?" Perhaps there are people lying in coffins all over the place waiting for God to reconnect.

AJ: I hope you're playing with me. I don't know who you are, but obviously, if you're out there, there must be something more than the boundaries of this box. And why would you have knocked? And you did say that I would be stuck here until processed, which implies that I might get unstuck in the future. Yes?

Gabriella: Look at that: some deductive logic from the astrophysicist. Now that we seem to have a point of understanding, let's focus on good news. You will be processed soon enough and then we can talk face to face about what happens next.

AJ: Next? Next on its own is such an ill-defined word. Is that next good or next bad? Or say next week, next year, next creation? The realms of possibility are endless. Perhaps you can give me just the extremes: the worst and the best possibilities.

Gabriella: Sorry, no realms of possibilities: only the two. We would say the better, a life in the presence of God – yes, there is one – or…

AJ: Or?

Gabriella: A life without God.

AJ: For how long?

Gabriella: Ever. Eternity. No end in time.

AJ: Is this a foregone conclusion for me?

Gabriella: Oh, no. God's mercy is infinite. There's always a chance of redemption. At the end of the process, you will have a choice. God or no God: no forcing, no cajoling, no intimidation, simply a choice.

AJ: Sounds too easy.

Gabriella: Yes, the process is simple, but the experience can be grueling.

AJ: When do we begin?

Gabriella: Soon.

AJ: *[Apprehensively.]* I know I should be grateful that we've come to some understanding, but truly, "What's with the processing?" Sounds very bureaucratic and that's not a word I have ever heard connected with any form of God. Everything should be instantaneous, if he's really omnipotent. Just trying to make a point.

Gabriella: It's she, not he. And, there's no bureaucracy; no checking files or computer printouts. The processing time is for you. Most people in your state think that they are dreaming – especially if they're not expecting consciousness after death. This period is allotted to give you the time to accept that this is not a dream – it's your new reality.

AJ: Does that work for everyone?

Gabriella: No, some spend a significant time in hell still thinking that they are dreaming. The difficulty, of course, is that when they finally admit to their new reality, it's too late to change their mind.

AJ: That sounds rather cruel. People get sent to hell because they think they are dreaming?

Gabriella: Choose to go; not sent. If after what you are going to go through, you think you're still dreaming, then nothing God can do will convince you otherwise. And between you and me, I've never actually heard it said out loud, but I think she has a big problem with vacillators.

AJ: So what do I do in the meantime – in this box?

Gabriella: Well, a wise person might take the time to reflect upon their earthly shortcomings – they will become important to remember. You will have to answer for all your transgressions – first to those you have harmed – and then to God herself.

AJ: I knew there had to be a catch. I'm not cut out for that self-reflective, touchy-feely crap – I've pretty much been right about things my whole life. *[Having an epiphany.]* I don't think I've ever apologized to anyone for anything.

Gabriella: Well, I guess you could simply spend the time thinking – you're supposed to be very good at that. I hear that contemplating on the next prime number can be very rewarding and time consuming; or what about that theory of everything problem, or dark matter or dark energy. Now that you have new experiential data about on-going consciousness, perhaps the equations can be adjusted. Oh, and maybe you can reflect upon your long-held opinions about God and religion; and, now that you know that there's life after death, you might try to figure out how you missed that. Seems like a rather significant error to me. *[Taps the coffin.]* See you in a bit.

AJ: Wait...wait...

[Gabriella ignores AJ's pleas and leaves the room.]

5
The Lobby Café, 1ˢᵗ Visit

Outside of an upscale coffee shop with an understated sign, **The Lobby Café, Always Open**, *there is a small patio with a few tables and chairs.*

Gabriella is sitting at one of the tables. She hears someone approaching, leans forward and waves. She stands up as AJ arrives. He is dressed in old track pants, a Grateful Dead t-shirt and flip-flops.

AJ: Gabriella?
Gabriella: *[Bows and laughs lightly.]* Nice outfit!
AJ: Those bastards – those supposed friends of mine. They always hated that I dressed so much better. I had everything planned – not that I was expecting to die, but I don't (should I say didn't?) leave things to chance. I had specific instructions for my exit – the viewing, the casket – already selected and paid for, of course. I wrote my own obituary. And my clothes: I was to be laid out in one of my best Saville Row suits wearing my Berluti handmade shoes. Can

you imagine the mockery at my viewing – wearing these? *[Points to his outfit.]* Those... those friends probably gave my entire wardrobe to some thrift store and now homeless people are walking around...

Gabriella: *[Sits down.]* Well it does seem like such a waste – being buried in expensive garments. It's not like you were expecting to meet anyone. And yet...

AJ: *[Changing the topic and sitting down across from Gabriella.]* I thought it was Gabriel?

Gabriella: Pardon?

AJ: Your name. I thought the archangel's name was Gabriel.

Gabriella: Archangels are androgynous – or gender fluid if you prefer.

AJ: What?

Gabriella: And asexual.

AJ: What a waste – you are stunning!

Gabriella: Don't get excited, your penis is merely an appendage here.

AJ: *[Looking down.]* Oh.

Gabriella: Yes! Disappointing? Especially for those suicide bombers. Lots of virgins but no sex. *[They both pause to regard each other for a moment.]* Let's see, it's been but a few minutes and the very frightened 'what kind of God' scientist, now free from his walnut casket, has reverted to his earthly self to hit on the angel. Nice move...did I mention that people rarely change here? *[Continuing.]* Anyway, as I was explaining, in your first encounter – which we call the examination of conscience – you will meet with those you failed to love while on earth.

AJ: Yes, yes, I get that part. I'm supposed to feel guilty about being a not-so-nice person – I'm sure my wives can hardly wait to have at me – but, I'm so much more interested in the second meeting with God himself.

Gabriella: *[Correcting.]* Herself.

AJ: *[Dismissively.]* Regardless…this meeting presents an appropriate intellectual challenge for me. The more I reflect upon it, the more exciting it becomes.

Gabriella: You might wish to approach these encounters with a more contrite mindset – at least give yourself a chance for redemption. Always remember two things: you will be incapable of lying, and in the end, you get to choose your final destiny.

AJ: I'm still not convinced that this isn't a dream. And, if not, I'm sure that I don't want to spend eternity in heaven – standing around praising God and singing alleluias or whatever it is you angels are purported to chant. Now, don't misunderstand me, I'm sure that might be better than spending eternity in some other place that bodes of punishment and repetition and heat and cold. At least I would think that heaven is temperature controlled. But, as I said at the beginning, I had a very good life on earth and I would be quite content to simply cease to exist.

Gabriella: We hear that a lot. And I suppose if there's a flaw in God's plan, it's the fact that once she endowed humankind with an immortal spirit, it couldn't be undone! Now, that may look like an error from your perspective, but believe me there are no bored souls in heaven.

AJ: Then those who choose heaven must be a simple lot. Doing the praise thing all day, every day, forever, simply won't work for me. Hell and all its nastiness sounds a lot like earth to me – bound to be more interesting and entertaining.

Gabriella: So the God who demanded so little of you on earth now becomes this narcissistic being who expects constant praise and worship from her minions. I wonder who that sounds like?

Here's the thing about God that you scientific guys don't comprehend. Most people who believe don't do so because of some Aquinian proof about the prime mover – that's the stuff of theologians and philosophers. They believe because they choose to. They look at creation and rightfully conclude that a loving creator is necessary for the whole thing to make sense.

AJ: Oh yes, we know: without God and religion, life has no meaning or purpose. 'We' would say that man makes his own purpose in life. I certainly did.

Gabriella: How does that concept work for the children of Yemen? Or the Rohingya? Or the refugees fleeing the Syrian civil war? Ignoring the shortcomings of that argument, what God imparts is this: universal justice. Since humankind first evolved, over 100 billion people have lived on earth. How many lived a life even remotely comparable to yours? How many died tragically from disease, violence, accident, hunger? How many were born with severe disabilities? How many were abandoned by those who were supposed to love them? Care to guess? For these, heaven is God's gift of perfect restorative justice. And in case you are wondering, God extends this gift to those who were fortunate in living a blest life on earth because her generosity is boundless, like her mercy.

AJ: If God were truly all merciful and all powerful, then *[emphasizing the 'she']* 'she' could have prevented all of those tragedies. Where was God when man was at his worst? *[Stops as he sees that Gabriella is smirking.]* You find this funny?

Gabriella: No, it's not funny; it's predictable. I had a wager with a colleague as to how long it would take you to bring up the 'God who watched human atrocities and did nothing' argument. Not long!

AJ: That doesn't invalidate the argument.

Gabriella: Ah, yes. The atheist who recoiled at the thought that God might simply be indifferent and leave him in his casket, now wants God the puppet master. You think God should have intervened in human affairs with great regularity to prevent humankind's atrocities on itself? Is that it?

Maybe you would be so kind as to tell us which evils God should have prevented? Wars? All wars or just the big ones? What about murders and school shootings? All of them or only those that involve children? What about traffic fatalities and of course sickness and disease? And are we talking about crimes only; what about sins – acts that caused great pain and suffering to others. Should God have inserted herself there? *[Moving to the edge of her seat, Gabriella displays a sense of real anger.]* Tell me professor, should God have inserted herself in the midst of all your adulterous exploits to save your wives from their pain and humiliation? What would have been the appropriate response in those situations? Maybe she should have caused your willy to fall off? What do you think about that?

AJ: *[A mite surprised by Gabriella's forcefulness, AJ switches the topic.]* But I don't need to be restored. I had a very good life on earth. No tragedies or major illnesses – not for me or my family. Save for my somewhat Epicurean lifestyle, I might have lived a few more years but then not so enjoyably. I have left the earth having tasted all of its pleasures and at the pinnacle of my career. No complaints!

Gabriella: And yet you too had a great reason for being a believer.

AJ: I don't follow.

Gabriella: All your life, you looked at the heavens and sought the answers to the universe's most complex mysteries. Having reached the 'pinnacle' of your profession, you entered the latter stages of your life and career without these answers: the resolution of relativity and quantum theory, the problems of dark matter and dark energy, the possibility of parallel universes. And despite this lifetime of searching, you approached death with zero chance of ever solving these queries. *[Pausing for effect – ensuring that AJ is paying attention.]* Your only hope for learning the answers to these mysteries lay in the existence of a creator who could reveal them in an afterlife. And yet you were content – no, not just content – but preferred to die into oblivion. And never know the solutions.

We find that strange!

[Gabriella stands and signals for AJ to do likewise. She goes to the door of the café, and then beckons AJ to follow her inside.]

The inside of the coffee shop is warm and hospitable. There are two clusters of tub chairs arranged around coffee tables, four wing-backed chairs flanking two open fireplaces and three round tables with accompanying chairs.

[Bishop Noonan and Mohammed are sitting at a table for four, drinking coffee and talking as Gabriella and AJ enter the café.]

Gabriella: You remind me of another astrophysicist who I guided through The Lobby in 1996 – Carl Sagan.

AJ: *[With a sudden renewed interest.]* You met Carl Sagan? Where is he now?

Gabriella: Oh, he's happily with God.

AJ: And he's not bored?

Gabriella: There's a large community of scientists in heaven. They meet regularly.

AJ: Who?

Gabriella: Who, what?

AJ: The scientists who meet – do you know their names?

Gabriella: Not all. I only know the ones that I have met… *[thinking]*…Galileo, Sagan, I mentioned, Newton, Currie, Fermi, Einstein…I haven't met him, but I heard that Stephen Hawking is now part of the group.

AJ: *[Astounded.]* Einstein is here? You've met him?

Dermot Nolan

Nolan, Ciarlo

1 King St West
Suite 700....

Desert Tiles

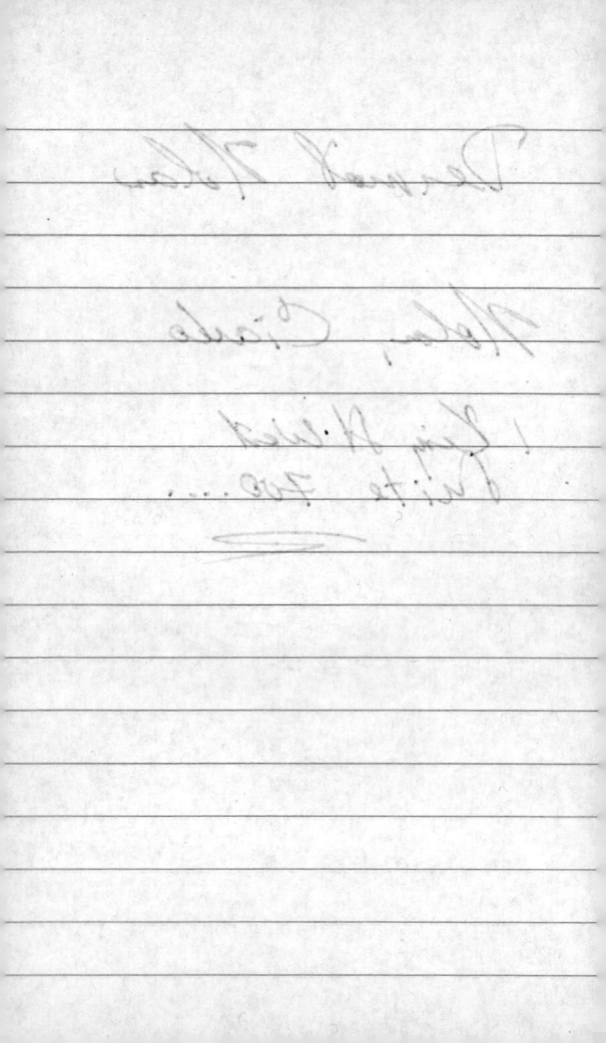

Maler Circle

King Field
White Pup

Gabriella: *[Playing indifferent.]* There are fifty billion people in heaven. Some of them were brilliant scientists on earth. Everyone has a story to tell, a secret to share, a mystery to be resolved.

AJ: *[Finally catching on.]* You mean the answers to all of the universe's mysteries are within my grasp? I'm that close to understanding the grand theory of everything?

Gabriella: *[Nonchalantly closing the distance to the table.]* There are no mysteries in heaven that are not shared. Not everyone is interested in the same things,of course, but there is endless knowledge available for those who wish to pursue it. Hell, on the other hand is adrift in ignorance.

[Mohammed waves.] Hey Mohammed!

AJ: Wait, I'm not finished… *[Gabriella and AJ face each other.]*

Gabriella: Later, perhaps.

AJ: Why not now?

Gabriella: We have more important issues to discuss.

[AJ and Bishop Noonan make eye contact and instantly recognize each other; AJ addresses Bishop Noonan.]

AJ: Whoa, cappa magna guy!

Bishop Noonan: *[Looks to Mohammed; Bishop Noonan is not happy.]* Why is he here?

Mohammed: Same reason as you.

Bishop Noonan: *[With disgust.]* Surely there are exceptions to the one-more-chance doctrine. There must be a go-straight-to-hell provision.

AJ: I'm standing right here! *[AJ looks at Mohammed and Bishop Noonan looks at Gabriella. AJ addresses Mohammed.]* And who might you be?

Mohammed: Mohammed.

AJ: Really? Seventh century guy?

Mohammed: Oh, no. Very distant relation. *[Looking at Bishop Noonan and then directing his focus to Gabriella.]* Paul, this is Gabriella.

[Bishop Noonan and Gabriella nod to each other.]

AJ: *[Addressing Bishop Noonan with a very big smirk. Bishop Noonan refuses to look at AJ.]* So, 'thee' Bishop Noonan, isn't this a pleasant surprise. You, with all your sacrifices: no women, no children, no house in the suburbs; and, all your Masses, fasting, incantations, etc. and, lo and behold, you're in the same situation as me – three wives, a serial philanderer, sometimes hard drinker and dedicated atheist. You didn't get the express treatment; you're on the maybe list. So what's the delay with your admission? You were actually diddling the altar servers yourself, not just covering up for the boys? *[Laughing loudly.]* I think I like this God.

Bishop Noonan: *[To Mohammed.]* I don't need to listen to this. *[Bishop Noonan begins to stand.]* Can't we continue our discussion elsewhere? I saw a prayer room down the hall.

Mohammed: You can leave, but your tolerance in the face of this tirade might help save him.

Bishop Noonan: *[Now standing and pointing at AJ.]* Nothing will save this man – he is not redeemable.

[Bishop Noonan abruptly leaves the café.]

Gabriella: *[Addressing Mohammed and AJ.]* Well, that went well. *[Pausing, to let the tension subside.]* As I was explaining to AJ about what happens next…

AJ: Don't think I've forgotten about meeting Einstein…and the process, as you have described it, is all wrong. You've been doing this for hundreds of years and you still don't have it right.

Mohammed: Well, you're welcome to tell us how to do it correctly, but you should know that despite the fact that you think you're the smartest person at the table and that you have maintained your argumentative self on this side of death, your ranting will be entirely one-sided. There's nothing we haven't heard before.

AJ: You've never heard from me before and perhaps I'm not only the smartest person at the table; perhaps I'm the smartest person you've ever met. *[Pausing.]* It's obvious that the meeting with God should come first. That way, we non-believers can be sure that this deity actually exists before we go through this conscience thing. Why should I get all worked up about meeting all the people I've supposedly wronged when it turns out that there is no God and I'm simply dreaming? *[AJ looks from person to person, looking for a response.]*

Mohammed: *[Mohammed and Gabriella share a glance.]* Tell you what AJ, we think you should tell God all about your misgivings about the process – right after you do your conscience thing. Now, shall we review the process one more time?

6
The Prayer Room

A magnificent space! A large circular room with a tented ceiling, well-lit by natural light flowing through floor to ceiling stained glass windows, reminiscent of a Marc Chagall design in blues and greens. The windows embody symbols of all religious beliefs and quotes in the original languages from sacred texts or oral traditions. There is a single pew in the centre of the room.

Bishop Noonan is seated on the pew, oblivious to his surroundings. AJ enters the room and speaks to Bishop Noonan.

AJ: Mind if I join you? *[AJ's voice seems to awaken Bishop Noonan and he is taken aback. He looks around to see who AJ is talking to and then realizes that he is the only other person in the room.]* I understand that you might rather be alone, but there doesn't seem to be any other place to go except the café and I'm not ready to talk to Gabriella. Well, that's not entirely true. I would like to talk to her about the chance to meet Einstein, but she keeps putting me off. All I hear about is this examination of conscience thing. Quite boring if you ask me.

Bishop Noonan: Sit, if you wish. *[They both sit quietly. An awkward silence.]* I don't care what Mohammed said, it's not going to be fair.

AJ: What did he say? What's not going to be fair?

Bishop Noonan: He said God wasn't fair. And, I'm saying this examination of conscience isn't going to be either.

AJ: I don't follow.

Bishop Noonan: They're going to come after me. They're going to say it was all my fault. *[Bishop Noonan seems to be in a state of shock and continues talking to no one. Just talking.]* All my life I've been one of the good ones. All my life I've been in love with the church. The whole idea behind it: the faith, the ceremonies, the history, the mysteries, the magnificence of the Easter Liturgy, or Midnight Mass at Christmas, or the Chrism Mass – have you ever attended a Chrism Mass – or an ordination or the election of a pope. The whole world still tunes into papal elections: the College of Cardinals, the Sistine Chapel and Michelangelo's paintings, the white smoke, the first appearance of the newly elected pontiff, the continuity of 2000 years of tradition. I love it. I have loved it. I will always love it.

You know, I started saying Mass – pretending – when I was eight or nine years old. My mother would always remind me that I did that, although I knew and remembered. She didn't need to remind me. I knew that I would be a priest from that very early time.

And, as I said, I was good. I don't mean at my job, but as a person. I kept the commandments – I never stole, I was good to my parents, I was never into material things, so the covet parts were never a temptation. I never fell in love or lust. Sometimes, I think I was asexual – although no one ever heard of that in those days. There were times when I could have fallen in love, but I chose not to. There was a young woman at university – second year history – we did a major project together. She was smart, beautiful and Jewish. Perhaps if she had been Catholic, it would have been different. But the Jewish part would never have worked – not for me; not for her. Also, when I was a young priest – an assistant at my first parish – there were young women in the parish and teachers in the parochial school who you just connected with. They were a temptation for me, but I simply willed the idea out of my life.

I was dedicated to God and to his church. I was smart too – very good with languages. They sent me to Rome to study, and I could have stayed to work at the Vatican; but, I was needed in my diocese, so I came home to middle class life and a parish of my own. It was the happiest time of my life. I was good at it! One day you're a pastor and then out of the blue, you get a call from the papal nuncio and he tells you that you are being elevated to bishop. And you're supposed to be humble about it. Try as you might – and regardless of the fact that you never strove to be a bishop – you do feel proud. Perhaps too proud. And everyone who loves you feels proud: your parents, siblings, and friends. It's hard not to be proud of yourself.

[Gets very animated.] Do you have any idea what it's like to be a bishop – when you actually get your own diocese? Foremost, nothing prepares you for the management of your priests. Understand that I loved my priests and their commitment to their mission and the faith and we were of one mind in the majority of issues, but their human personalities can be a nightmare. "I can't work with that guy;" "If you transfer me to that parish, I will retire." Or how about this one: "Do you know that he (the previous pastor) signed the organist to a ten year contract the week before I was to take over – and the guy can't play and everyone in the choir hates him."

Every phone call to a bishop is a problem! No one calls to tell you that you're doing a great job. No, the conservatives call to complain about Vatican

II and why won't I say Mass in Latin or protest some fundraiser in support of a Catholic agency that has a pro-choice politician as the guest speaker and can't I remove the word "Catholic" from their name; and, then some liberal wants to know why his gay son can't be married in the Cathedral.

I was never cut out for running a diocese. You need to be a good administrator and you need a head for business.

AJ: Or surround yourself with good people and then delegate.

Bishop Noonan: Yes, that would have been helpful, but priests don't necessarily know those things – they're not taught in the seminary. *[Puts his head in his hands.]* And then it began. Rumours and whispers of improper conduct by my priests with children. I was shocked to the core. I couldn't believe it. No Catholic priest would do such a thing. It was the work of the devil himself – lies to sow discord in the church. This was my church and I would protect it with my life. I simply refused to accept that 'these stories' were possible.

In the end, for the most part, I ignored it. I told my chancellor to deal with it and he did. He investigated, of course, a lot of "he said, he said" stuff. And we spoke to the best psychologists of the time and they told us it was not such a big deal – a stint in a treatment centre for the priest and there would be no permanent harm to the children. So those who admitted to improprieties...

AJ: Improprieties? Really?

Bishop Noonan: You weren't there. We had no experience in dealing with this issue. We followed the advice of those who were supposed to know. We sent the priests to a treatment centre and they were treated for a year or so and then we put them back into ministry.

AJ: *[With some exasperation.]* But didn't you involve the police? These actions were in fact crimes.

Bishop Noonan: *[Responding in kind.]* Not officially. We had to follow canon law and informing secular authorities about offending priests was not allowed. We had, of course, police officers and lawyers who were very active in the church with whom we discussed these things – not specific cases but generalities. We were told not to worry. You must understand that my job was to protect the church. Its reputation was more important than the sins of a few bad apples. I did the best I could.

AJ: *[Attempting to shift the tone.]* Tell me then Paul... *[looks to see if using his first name draws any reaction from Bishop Noonan – it does not]*...from this account, you seemed to be a rather low key person. How did you end up as the Cappa Magna guy? Why the sudden adoption of all the pomp and circumstance of the church? If you were not ambitious, why accept the transfer to Rome?

Bishop Noonan: I wanted out and I think the Vatican was afraid I was going to break down and say more than I should. Believe me, it was a relief. It took me away from all the problems in the diocese. I embraced the church in Rome. It was an opportunity to rid myself of the nastiness of real life and lose myself in the glorified history and ceremony of Rome and the Vatican. I deserved it. I had been the good and faithful servant; why not relish every moment?

AJ: Ah, that I understand. The spotlight is seductive; erotic in fact. Best sex ever.

Bishop Noonan: I wouldn't know.

AJ: Well I think you do. Nothing beats dressing up in a $5000 suit and listening to the applause of your peers as they praise you for your accomplishments. It may be fleeting, but in that moment it's an orgasm of the soul. I can picture you wearing that flowing cape with your priestly vestments while walking up the aisle in that magnificent cathedral, with every eye in the church fixed on you – that would be intoxicating. *[Both of them sit staring forward. Then AJ continues, simply matter-of-factly.]*

Anything strange been happening to you? My memory of life on earth has returned with a vengeance. I remember names, places and conversations – some are good but many are not so flattering. I can't believe some of the things I said and did. Although I'm somewhat taken aback, I can't say as I ever felt guilty about anything. Regret of course, but even that, not too often. I suppose this memory reboot is to prepare us for our meetings with those we have offended. Have you given any thought as to whom you will meet?

Bishop Noonan: *[Depressed.]* Why should it be any different here than when I was on earth? Any queries about my past always began with the child abuse scandal. My whole life was compacted into those years when I was a bishop. Nothing else mattered. I expect that I will meet the victims. And they will pummel me for my failure to do more. It will be so unfair…

AJ: *[Continuing as before; not really paying attention to Bishop Noonan.]* I suppose my first wife might try to make me feel guilty about the children – how I never had time for them. And how they needed a father. Well, my parents never played with me – sent me off to boarding school for ten months of the year and then summer camp for two. And look how well I responded – top of my class and top of my profession. Of course, there was also lots of sex – particularly with my grad students – but they were all of age and I bored of wives two and three quite quickly.

And then there were my polemics against the stupid and the weak, but I had no time for those less than myself – I never suffered fools. And look at the God thing. Should I feel guilty because she couldn't reveal herself to me? I'm perceptive, observant, curious – yet I never found God. Seems she came up short in her plan, if it was to get me to pay attention.

Well, whatever happens, I've always been ready for a good argument. I do think, however, that there will be no "I don't remember" answers permitted. And pleading the fifth or attempts at outright lying probably won't work in this particular situation. *[Rubbing his hands, and moving his tongue about.]* My tongue is a little dry and my hands are starting to sweat. Why do you suppose that is?

Bishop Noonan: In a few moments, we are going to be on trial. And the outcome will determine how we live out eternity.

AJ: *[Finally sensing the seriousness of it all.]* Oh, right.

Bishop Noonan: Shall we join our keepers and see what advice they have to offer.

[Bishop Noonan and AJ leave the prayer room and head back to the café.]

7
The Lobby Café, 2nd Visit

Inside the café their table has two piles of notes and file folders, some loose papers and pens.

AJ and Bishop Noonan enter the café and approach the table expecting to see Mohammed and Gabriella. They both look around and then focus on the table and its collection of papers.

Bishop Noonan: *[While still standing, Bishop Noonan picks up a note from the table and reads.]* "We have left some material to assist with your examinations of conscience. We think that these excerpts may prepare you for what is to come. However, no one can ever be sure what will happen: who you will meet, what questions you might be asked. We have an additional recommendation for AJ. As people who dream are incapable of reading aloud, we suggest you read the highlighted sections to each other. It would be beneficial if AJ could approach this next phase convinced that this is not a dream. Sincerely, Gabriella and Mohammed"

AJ: *[Grabs note and reads silently.]* Dumb! The whole thing is dumb.

Bishop Noonan: *[Resigned.]* Let's just get this over.

AJ: Fine. You read mine and I'll read yours. *[Both take a seat at the table and sort through the material until they each have the pile that they want.]*

Bishop Noonan: Do you wish to go first?

AJ: Sure, bring it on!

Bishop Noonan: *[Reading from a document.]* Let's see…according to a survey conducted by the Johns Hopkins School of Public Health, "As many as 654,965 more Iraqis may have died since hostilities began in Iraq in March 2003 than would have been expected under pre-war conditions."[1] *[Flipping the page over, looking for additional details.]* Is that a typo: 654,000?

AJ: *[Standing abruptly, trying to comprehend, then gets it.]* So that's it. I'm to be held accountable for my vocal support of that war. I knew this place would be full of liberals. Well that report is bunk; it's been dismissed as seriously flawed. *[Now seeing his opportunity.]* Damn, I'm really looking forward to debating whoever heaven has to offer regarding the correctness of that war.

Bishop Noonan: *[Still looking at the document.]* But 654,000? Could that possibly be true?

AJ: I have no idea and neither does the Johns Hopkins School of Public Health. And whatever the numbers, they are deceiving because they include soldiers, Iraqi police officials, people killed in car bombings by insurgents and even those who died from illnesses caused by infrastructure damage – contaminated water...

Bishop Noonan: Still that's a lot of people that would have not otherwise have died – Yes?

AJ: Liberals love to study things to death, but they are afraid of getting their hands dirty to actually solve problems. In war, people die. And Saddam Hussein was a tyrant of the first order and the world is better off without him.

Bishop Noonan: Simply being curious, what is your estimate of the number of – say, only civilians – who were killed by the Americans?

AJ: Invading armies don't count the civilians they kill. General Tommy Franks said, "We don't do body counts!"

Bishop Noonan: But others have published articles, like this study – surely there is a minimum number that most agree upon?

AJ: I don't know, probably around fifteen thousand, plus or minus. *[Taking a pause.]* Now, what else do you have to share?

Bishop Noonan: *[Picking up another document.]* This is a passage from a book entitled *A War Against Truth*.

[Bishop Noonan reads to himself, digesting the content as he flips back and forth over a couple of pages.] Let me summarize for you. The author is speaking to an Iraqi doctor about the impact of the shock and awe bombing tactic upon the children of Baghdad. The doctor is quoted as saying that over two hundred thousand children will be permanently scarred – suffering from fear and anxiety for the balance of their lives.[2] What say you to that, Mr. Humanitarian?

AJ: Are you done? *[Bishop Noonan nods.]* So, war is hell. Not my fault. If God were so good and powerful, she... *[looking around and above, and with great emphasis]*...she should have done something about it. And it just occurred to me, you Catholics love to quote from Augustine, do you not? Isn't he the guy who proposed the 'just war theory'. Perhaps someone should talk to him. *[Speaking again to the heavens.]* And if you're so concerned about the welfare of children, please tell me that this guy... *[pointing at Bishop Noonan]*...and all those like him will follow me into hell for their abuse and cover up. At least in war, the children are not specifically targeted. They're just collateral damage.

Bishop Noonan: Thanks, that was nice! What happened to the "can I join you Paul" person?

AJ: Oh, and the Mr. Humanitarian comment wasn't a dig? And by the way, what nobody-ever-heard-of-author wrote that nobody-ever-heard-of book? I hope there's something more impressive in the remaining crib notes than these two weak-assed offerings. Boy, this is dull and boring.

Bishop Noonan: Well let's see if we can spice it up a little just for you. *[Switching to a more animated role, playing the role of game show host.]* OK, Bob, what do we have next for the eminent astrophysicist – something a little more challenging for his mighty intellect? *[Flipping through a couple of papers, he picks up a single sheet of paper, reads it over and smiles.]* What do we have on the board? Famous quotes for $200. Name the author and the book.

[Reading.] "On the whole, men are more good than bad; that, however, isn't the real point. But they are more or less ignorant, and it is this that we call vice or virtue; the most incorrigible vice being that of an ignorance that fancies it knows everything and therefore claims for itself the right to kill."[3] *[Bishop Noonan starts making beeping noises, like a game show timer.]* Do, do, do, do, do, do, do, do…remember, you're answer has to be in the form of a question…do, do, do, do…

AJ: *[Getting into Jeopardy mode.]* Wait, I know this…Algerian guy…I got it! What is *The Plague* by Albert Camus? *[Bishop Noonan signals with a 'ding, ding' – the winner. AJ and Bishop Noonan regard each other in this silliness and quickly resume their usual* *attitudes.]* Good quote, but it can't apply in war. People die, soldiers and civilians; it's what happens. Get over it! And if Camus is to be my adversary in this examination of conscience, then agreement or not, the intellectual challenge will be exhilarating. What else?

Bishop Noonan: *[Flipping through a few more pages.]* Mostly, more of the same. I think you're as ready as you're going to get. Perhaps this one last quote might instill some sense of humility in you – a quality more appropriate for the situation. *[Reading from another document.]* "For the barbarian is the man who regards his passions as their own excuse for being; who does not domesticate them… His delight is in abundance and vehemence…His scorn for what is poorer and weaker than himself is only surpassed by his ignorance of what is higher."[4] Wow. That pretty much describes you.

AJ: Ha, ha…you're right, an apt description for me. I accept. Is there an award for being a barbarian? I rather liked the prose; who is the author? *[Takes the document from Bishop Noonan. Reads and turns page, until he finds what he is looking for.]* Oh, how disappointing, Santayana. A rather mediocre philosopher. *[AJ stares at Bishop Noonan, who shrugs his shoulders to indicate that there are no more notes for AJ.]*

Bishop Noonan: That's it.

AJ: How disappointing! Nothing about the missteps of my personal life, save the barbarian comment – the person who does not domesticate his passions. It seems I'm to be judged solely on my support for this one war. Not much of a challenge. Actually, I'm rather looking forward to my adversaries. If I'm going to hell, I may as well have some fun on the way. *[AJ now realizes that it is his turn to read. He sits down and gathers together the pages pertaining to Bishop Noonan. He looks at Bishop Noonan to see if he is ready.]*

Bishop Noonan: Before you start, let me guess. I'm about to have my own shock and awe moment regarding my failure to address the sexual abuse of children by priests in my diocese. You are going to read about my refusal to acknowledge what was going on; the fact that I didn't report accusations to the police; that I was more concerned about the reputation of the church than about the well-being of the children; that I simply fulfilled the orders of the Vatican. Well, I've heard all this before – hundreds of times and my answers will be the same as I've given in the past. *[AJ, having heard all this before, silently mouths the next three sentences.]* I didn't know then what I know now. The psychologists said that the priests could be cured; that it wasn't such a big deal – that the children wouldn't be scarred. I was a bishop and I had to follow the orders of my superiors – the Vatican has rules.

AJ: *[Looking astounded.]* That's your defence: you had to follow rules? You're actually going to say you choose the church over the children?

Bishop Noonan: It's not that simple. The Roman Catholic Church conducts its business through the rigorous application of canon law – versions of which have existed since the 5th century.

AJ: Of course we mustn't let justice interfere with the rule of law.

Bishop Noonan: I'm not sure that the warmonger merits the right to comment on the virtue of justice.

AJ: Even a vegetarian can identify a cow.

Bishop Noonan: Stupid comment. *[Pausing.]* Yes, I protected the church. Don't looked so astonished. Organizations protect themselves from scandal; that's how they survive. Look at Penn State and Joe Paterno.

AJ: Oh yes, great example. Look how that worked out. And, shouldn't the church have set a higher bar.

Bishop Noonan: *[Leaning forward and pointing his finger at AJ.]* Did I interrupt you when you were ranting about war and children? Listen to Mr. Collateral Damage! I did my best. I have a clear conscience! *[AJ and Bishop Noonan are now visibly angry. AJ picks up the first paper, peruses and begins to read aloud.]*

AJ: *[Somewhat smugly.]* Something entitled *The Book of Gomorrah*, written by St. Peter Damian circa 1049 – let's see what our friends have highlighted for your examination. *[Gets animated and mimics some of the described punishments.]* "A cleric or monk who seduces youths or young boys…is to be publicly flogged and lose his tonsure. When his hair has been shorn, his face is to be foully besmeared with spit and he is to be bound in iron chains. For six months he will languish in prison-like confinement and on three days of each week shall fast on barley bread in the evening."[5] What, no year in rehab at a cushy resort and reassignment to a new parish?

Let's see what else this document has to offer? Excellency, I think you'll find this part very informative. Good Saint Damien also has a few words *[with emphasis on the next three words]* specifically for bishops: "Let the indolent superiors of clerics and priests hear; let them hear and let them greatly fear being participants in the guilt of others…those who close their eyes to the correction of their subordinates' sins and offer them the freedom of sinning through *[with great emphasis]* an ill-advised silence. Let them hear…that they all equally deserve death…"[6] Wow. Only written, what, 1000 years ago? You are screwed! *[Bishop Noonan simply looks down with his head in his hands. AJ continues.]*

What do we have next? It seems to be an op-ed piece from a local newspaper – I would assume something from your own diocese. Let's see. It says here and I quote: "In this jurisdiction, with the passing of the Child Protection Act of 1984, every teacher, recreation director and camp counsellor knew full well their duty with respect to suspected cases of child abuse – any and all cases were to be reported to the local police or child welfare agency. The act applied to the clergy as well. Why didn't they know and comply?"[7] Why not indeed? 1984 – was that not well before some of your own cases? It's looking worse for you every moment. *[AJ picks up additional pages.]* Let's see what other gems might be here.

Bishop Noonan: *[Stands up abruptly, points his finger at AJ.]* That's it! You've had your fun at my expense, you smug bastard. I told you what would be in those papers for me, you don't need to rub it in. I don't need pontification from the likes of you. *[Looking upward to heaven and pointing a finger.]* I was your good and loyal servant. "Why have you forsaken me?"[8]

[Looking completely defeated, Bishop Noonan leaves the café, with AJ at the table still reading some papers.]

8
The Court Room, Bishop Noonan

The court room is intimidating; it is an appropriate space for an examination of conscience. This is not a room for the determination of guilt or innocence. Every deed exposed in this room has already been decreed by God, herself, as an act of wrongdoing. The guilty verdict has already been delivered. The room is a virtual IMAX theatre, with a large curved screen stretching from floor to ceiling – perhaps forty feet high. There are no seats. There is a witness box situated at the focal point of the screen and a solitary prie-dieu set some distance removed.

Mohammed enters the room with a prayer rug rolled under his arm. He lays out the rug near the witness box and begins to pray. A few minutes later, Bishop Noonan enters the room. He looks confused.

Bishop Noonan: You are at prayer? Even here?

Mohammed: *[Looking up but still on his knees.]* Someone is always in need of prayer.

Bishop Noonan: *[Not registering Mohammed's comment; pointing to the witness box.]* Do I stand there?

Mohammed: Yes...and Paul, a suggestion. *[Bishop Noonan looks at Mohammed.]* It might be wise to shed some of that clerical garb – perhaps go with the cassock only.

Bishop Noonan: *[Annoyed with the suggestion.]* Why? Should I be embarrassed about being a bishop?

Mohammed: No. But simplicity and humility will serve you better. *[Bishop Noonan, ignoring Mohammed's suggestion, moves to the witness stand. He is very uncomfortable – not sure where to look or where to put his hands.]* May God be with you Paul.

[A solitary woman (Theresa de Delores) appears on the massive screen. She resembles a street person with hair askew, dirty clothes, multiple tattoos and body piercings.]

Theresa: Bishop.

Bishop Noonan: *[Looking very puzzled as to whom this is.]* Should I know you?

Theresa: Theresa. Theresa de Delores.

Bishop Noonan: *[Looking quite shaken.]* I'm sorry... *[Lost for words.]*

Theresa: *[Theresa's questioning is not nasty, rather very perfunctory.]* Lost for words, Bishop? Quite a transition wouldn't you say? I take it you don't know what happened to me after we last met? I've had quite the life since you interviewed me about Father Raymond. Would you like the ten second summary? *[Theresa doesn't wait for a reply.]* First, I tried to lose myself in academia, including three years in law school. Didn't work! Then two failed marriages. Do you have any idea how difficult it is to be intimate with someone you love when any type of touching makes you want to vomit? Couldn't hold a job, in and out of drug rehab, eventually living on the street with a couple of suicide attempts. Fortunately for me the third try was successful as I'm now at peace. Being called a liar about Father Raymond's abuse – first by my parents, then our pastor, the principal and finally you – really did a thing to my head. I knew that I hadn't made it up, so it must have been my fault.

Bishop Noonan: I'm sorry, Theresa. I've apologized a thousand times. I can't go back and make you whole.

Theresa: No, but now you might get some appreciation for the depth of the hurt you caused. *[Pauses to let the idea sink in.]* We will begin with a review of your governance of the diocese. How long were you bishop?

Bishop Noonan: *[Perturbed.]* I knew this was going to happen! Is this really necessary?

Theresa: Yes. It is. Please answer the question.

Bishop Noonan: *[Sighing.]* Twenty-six years.

Theresa: And how many of your priests were convicted of the sexual abuse of children?

Bishop Noonan: *[Very quietly.]* Twenty-two.

Theresa: Bishop, you must speak up when you are answering questions. So how many?

Bishop Noonan: Twenty-two.

Theresa: And how many lawsuits have been settled for these twenty-two?

Bishop Noonan: Ninety-seven.

Theresa: And how many of those priests did you as the head of the diocese actually report to the local authorities?

Bishop Noonan: None.

Theresa: In our diocese after 1984 was there not a legal requirement to report all accusations of child abuse to either the child welfare agency or the local police?

Bishop Noonan: I know that now, but I was not aware of the law at the time.

Theresa: Is ignorance of the law an acceptable excuse?

Bishop Noonan: I can't go back and change what I didn't know.

Theresa: Didn't the diocese have competent legal representation responsible for keeping you abreast of any changes in the law that affected the operation of the corporation? Didn't the national conference of Catholic Bishops educate their members about these new legal reporting requirements?

Bishop Noonan: Look, I only know that I didn't know. Maybe others in the diocese were aware. The diocese was a big operation; there were many employees.

Theresa: And no one briefed you?

Bishop Noonan: No.

Theresa: So what does that say about the corporate culture under your leadership?

Bishop Noonan: Pardon?

Theresa: Were your people – your chancellor, vicar-general, diocesan lawyers – led to believe that these issues were to be handled by them and you were not to be involved?

Bishop Noonan: No, never.

Theresa: So how could you not know? You had many diocesan youth programs, including several children's camps that fully briefed their teenage staff on this law and their duty to report. And you're telling me that these young people were better informed regarding child abuse reporting protocols than the chief shepherd of the diocese?

Bishop Noonan: *[Forcefully.]* My job was to protect the church. I didn't know what camp counsellors were supposed to do. I regarded the priesthood as the pinnacle of human callings and that Catholic priests did not abuse children. Now I may have been wrong in anticipating that all priests were like me, but I approached the problem from that perspective.

I now know that I was wrong, but at the time I felt that I was doing the right thing. And don't forget the psychologists were telling us that this condition was treatable, and in fact, curable. Further, that the harm to the children would be minimal. I trusted their opinions. We honestly didn't know.

Theresa: You didn't know what? That sodomizing children was horribly wrong? That asking little girls to perform fellatio was not criminal? If at the time you didn't know and now you do, where do you lay the blame for this scandal? Where does the fault lie?

Bishop Noonan: On the priests themselves. Everything in their behavior was antithetical to their calling. What they did was disgusting – both to the children and to the church. And the secular media. They made a circus out of this entire scandal. They love to bring down the church every chance they get

Theresa: Maybe then you could explain these actions. In response to one of the lawsuits, your diocesan legal team blamed both parents and the children for contributing to the abuse. "The negligence of the Plaintiffs contributed to cause the injury or damage…" [*Bishop Noonan tries to reply but Theresa cuts him off.*] Please wait until I'm finished. And your vicar-general gave this comment to the local papers, "… the sexual assault victims and their parents share responsibility for the abuse. No one ever says anything about what the role of the parents was in all of this..." and he continued his spree by saying that the plaintiffs, who were as young as nine when the abuse began, "... knew what was right and what was wrong. Anybody who reaches the age of reason shares responsibility for what they do."

Bishop Noonan: The vicar-general was not speaking on behalf of the diocese and the comments in the lawsuit were not of my doing. The lawyers and the insurance companies required such statements in order to protect the diocese from bankruptcy. I had responsibilities other than responding to the needs of the victims. The whole diocese was in danger of financial ruin.

Theresa: Did you think the children were to blame?

Bishop Noonan: No, of course not. I'm not a monster!

Theresa: The parents?

Bishop Noonan: *[Hesitating slightly.]* No.

Theresa: So why didn't you instruct your lawyers and insurance people to simply remove those statements?

Bishop Noonan: It was just the way things were done and I was not one to rock the boat.

Theresa: Did you arrive at this course of action on your own, or were you directed by the Vatican?

Bishop Noonan: I'm not sure what you mean?

Theresa: Did the Vatican have a specific policy with regard to the reporting of priests who were suspected of child sexual abuse?

Bishop Noonan: *[Bishop Noonan takes out a handkerchief and wipes his brow and then his whole face. He begins to speak, then hesitates. When he does speak, his voice is trembling.]* It was forbidden to report a priest to the police. *[Taking a couple of deep breaths, Bishop Noonan continues in his shaky voice.]* Until the promulgation of the 1983 Code of Canon Law, it was forbidden under threat of excommunication. *[Pausing again.]* It wasn't until 2010 that bishops throughout the world were directed to comply with domestic laws.

Theresa: Bishop, would you say that these were well known facts?

Bishop Noonan: No.

Theresa: You do realize that the cover up has been almost as evil as the abuse. Your denials made the victims liars and drove many, including me, to drug abuse and suicide. And if your goal was to save the church from scandal, you have failed miserably at that as well. This scandal has now endured for over fifty years and has driven away many believers from the fold. Lastly, your failure to act has tainted every good priest with suspicion. The priesthood has become the butt of jokes for comedians and talk show hosts.

Bishop Noonan: *[Frustrated. Speaks slowly.]* Yes, we failed. We had no idea how serious the problem was at the time. We did our best.

Theresa: Bishop, once it became obvious that you had been deceived by your priests and that you had completely mishandled the response, why didn't you resign? Why didn't the whole lot of you resign? Why didn't the leadership of the church admit to failure and collectively step aside.

Bishop Noonan: I didn't fail. I acted as a bishop should and I don't have a bad conscience for what I did. I can't speak for the other bishops; I can only assume that they felt as I did. It would not have been fair for us bishops to be punished for things we didn't do. We did not abuse the children.

Theresa: So you were in charge of your diocese when twenty-two priests abused ninety-seven children – which became part of one of the greatest scandals in the 2000 year history of the church and you and your fellow bishops did nothing wrong. Aside from the fact that this statement is beyond belief, are you not the followers of Jesus of Nazareth – the man you claim was unjustly accused, tortured and murdered? Surely if you were to emulate your savior, you would have cheerfully sacrificed your careers for the good of the church. *[Looks painfully at Bishop Noonan who offers no reply.]* I guess not!

One last observation Bishop. You said you've apologized a thousand times... *[Bishop Noonan goes to answer, but Theresa cuts him off]*...but were you ever disciplined by the church? Were you demoted? Actually, you got a promotion. You got to leave the country and escape the people and the media where you were best known. Were you ever threatened with being laicized? Were you admonished and sent to a monastery to live out your life in prayer and reflection? Were you ever arrested, finger-printed or put on trial? Did you spend even so much as one day in jail? *[Bishop Noonan's head remains bowed.]*

No, the answer to all of the above is a big and loud NO. *[With added emphasis.]* But, you apologized a thousand times. Well Bishop, my time with you is over. It saddens me that you refuse to take ownership of this scandal in our diocese. Perhaps you will be more forthcoming with the other victims. *[Screen goes dark and Theresa is gone.]*

Bishop Noonan: *[Yelling at the dark screen while looking around for assistance.]* What other victims? This isn't over? I didn't know. I acted as a bishop should. I don't have a bad conscience for what I did.

[Bishop Noonan, alone on the witness stand, awaits the next victim.]

9
The Court Room, AJ

The court room is empty. Bishop Noonan has completed his examination of conscience.

Gabriella enter the room and kneels at the prie-dieu. Shortly thereafter, AJ arrives and goes immediately to the witness box.

AJ: *[Surveying the room, AJ seems quite affected by the surroundings. He sounds a little hyper.]* Never been to court. So this is what it's like. Rather impressive! How do you think I'll do?

Gabriella: *[After a moment she looks up from her prayer.]* We don't make predictions. We are forever hopeful that each sinner will have an awakening – a recognition that they could have loved so much better than they did.

AJ: *[Focusing on Gabriella.]* Well I think that's doubtful for me. *[The screen comes alive with the image of a woman, Maggie Forsythe. She is dressed in jeans, plaid shirt and squall jacket. She is wearing muddy hiking* boots. *She looks very healthy with rosy cheeks and wind-blown hair. For a moment AJ fails to see her as he is still focused on Gabriella. AJ turns and sees her, but there is a delay in recognition.]* Maggie? Maggie is that you? What are you doing here?

Maggie: Alex, what are you wearing?

AJ: A joke by my supposed friends. It was quite depressing at first, but I've gotten used to it now. *[Tenderly.]* No one has called me that for a long time. You and my mother were the only ones who ever called me Alex. I'd forgotten. You look great by the way – your skin is glowing! Have you been hiking?

Maggie: Yes, I've had quite the invigorating day.

AJ: *[Now remembering where he is.]* Oh they're so very good at throwing you off your game here. I had taken them at their word that my support of the Iraq War would be the focus of this trial and now you show up. You know me, Margaret, I have never backed away from a good argument. My hope is that they're sending their very best to be my adversary – Augustine perhaps or someone more recent. But…you've been sent out to distract me. While I'm punching holes in their do-good concept of human history, I'll suddenly be sidelined from my arguments by thoughts about what an asshole I was as a husband. I must admit that I wasn't expecting anything so underhanded from these so-called saints. How naïve I've been, thinking everything they've said would be on the up and up.

Maggie: *[Somewhat exasperated.]* No Alex, you are wrong!

AJ: Wrong, Margaret? Never!

Maggie: Alex, I'm not here to take you off your game by making you contemplate the shortcomings of your personal affairs; and, although an 'I'm sorry' to all the women you shafted will be an eventual requirement for your entry into this place – believe me that will be your easiest apology. No, I'm here to caution you – this trial will not be what you expect. It will be hard and long. Your endurance will be tested and your soul will be stripped bare. Your intellect will be challenged as never before – and not by an argument of esoteric quality but by one of severe simplicity. Alex, I and all the hosts of heaven are praying for your conversion. *[The screen goes dark and Maggie is gone.]*

AJ: What, no goodbye? *[Looking somewhat bemused.]* Is that it? *[While AJ is looking around for Gabriella and recognizing that he is alone, the screen comes alive again with a family of four: a Muslim woman (Mariam) dressed in an abaya and hijab, carrying a baby in her arms. With her are two other children, a toddler asleep in a stroller, and a pre-teen girl.]*

Mariam: Dr. Forsythe.

AJ: Yes? I don't know you madam, nor, I surmise these... *[pointing to the children]*...your children? I'm sure that we have never encountered each other before. I would have remembered.

Mariam: My name is Mariam and you are correct – these are my children. *[Pointing to each child.]* Fatima was ten; Abdullah had just turned three; and the baby, his name is Omar. We have not met face-to-face before, but we were the recipients of a gift from America on March 20, 2003. A cruise missile!

Fatima was the most fortunate – she was decapitated and died instantly. Abdullah was not so fortunate. He was in the next room when the missile hit and he took two days to die – suffering from intolerable pain the entire time, while calling out for me. The baby and I were trapped for three days in the rubble of the building. He died soon after our rescue. I succumbed to my injuries a few days later. I'm not sure if I actually died as a result of the missile or from the broken heart of losing all my children or from the anguish of hearing Abdullah cry out to me and my inability to comfort him in his suffering.

So you see Dr. Forsythe, we are acquainted. We are the collateral damage of your war.

AJ: *[His smugness now gone; he seems somewhat bewildered.]* I have no answer for your tragedy save that we – the U.S. – made every effort to ensure that only military installations and necessary infrastructure were targeted for our ordnance. We did our utmost to limit civilian casualties and we were, of course, troubled when we did not achieve this goal.

Mariam: Really? Did you accurately report the number of civilian deaths? Was there a story in the *New York Times*, "Mother and her three children killed by cruise missile strike"? Did the paper run our pictures? Did Americans get to see the decapitated body of my ten year old daughter? Or were we simply listed as collateral damage in the early days of the war? Or worse yet, was there nothing at all to say about our four lives – were we not counted at all?

You say that you were troubled – what does that mean? Sounds to me like the 'thoughts and prayers' that you Americans send to your victims of mass shootings. Words and no actions. For most of you, war is an abstraction. It happens to other people in other places. Killing is sterile: no people, no blood, no bodies, no rotting flesh. Well, for you this will now change! You will get to experience the war you so enthusiastically supported. You will get to meet the civilians who died for your cause. Then you can watch them die.

AJ: I will watch them die?

Mariam: Yes, starting with my family.

AJ: How many am I to witness?

Mariam: How many did you tell the Bishop – 15,000?

AJ: *[Visibly shaken and getting angry.]* That's obscene!

Mariam: *[Responding in kind.]* Please spare us your righteous anger. Dropping bombs is obscene. Observing the results of your actions is history. Who gave you the right to decide that some shall die and some shall live? And how dare you then state that the witnessing of the results of your decision is wrong! Do it; just don't tell me about it or let me see it. This is moral cowardice. *[Pausing, finished with her rant.]* Dr. Forsythe, do you have children?

AJ: Yes.

Mariam: Adult children, perhaps with families of their own? How many of your children or grandchildren died in this war? Were wounded? Now suffer from PTSD? Surely someone as vocal in his support of this war had children serving in the U.S. military. Tell me that you risked someone you love in offering your support.

AJ: *[Simply shakes his head.]*

Mariam: No one? So, in this game of life, my family went all in while you only played with your words. You risked nothing. *[Pausing as Fatima, the ten year old tugs at her mother's sleeve. They have an aside conversation.]* Fatima has a question for you. She would like to know why America thought it was good to kill her family?

AJ: *[Directing his reply to Mariam.]* America didn't set out... *[AJ is interrupted mid-sentence by Mariam.]*

Mariam: *[Forcefully.]* Answer the child Dr. Forsythe, it's her question.

AJ: *[AJ tries to find some words, but simply mutters.]*

Mariam: What, no sophisticated reply? It's a simple question. *[AJ averts his gaze.]* I guess not. *[There is a whistle of a falling bomb. Everyone looks skyward.]* Our conversation is over and it is time for you to begin your ordeal. You will remember us, Dr. Forsythe; you will remember our names; you will never again refer to us as collateral damage.

[Loud explosion, burst of light.]

10
The Lobby Café, 3rd Visit

Inside The Lobby Café Bishop Noonan and Mohammed are sitting at their table. Bishop Noonan looks completely tattered – hair and beard showing two months growth. He is wearing only the black cassock with fuchsia piping, which looks like it has been slept in. He is angry.

Bishop Noonan: [*Directing his anger at Mohammed, Bishop Noonan starts to talk but can't find his words. He slumps in his chair and then starts again.*] That was cruel. I did not deserve to be questioned in that manner. Did you see what they did? [*Mohammed nods, but does not answer.*] Of course you did! And you were absolutely no help at all. [*Bishop Noonan pushes back his chair, stands and shakes his finger at Mohammed.*] Ninety-seven! Incredible! Ninety-seven – that's how many victims confronted and questioned me! And… [*loudly*]…do you know how many of those people I abused? None! Not any of them. I was given the task of cleaning up the mess of others. And did I get any thanks? Not one word.

And the questions – they were all the same. Why did I not call the police? Why did I not fire the priests? Why did I not do this? Why did I not do that? I did investigate the complaints that were brought to my attention but the evidence was never conclusive. Their stories were not consistent; they couldn't remember important details, dates and times; they were often not able to describe what had happened. How could I take these inconsistencies to the police or suspend a priest from his ministry over what often sounded like harmless affections? I was never fully convinced that the priests were truly guilty.

Mohammed: *[Somewhat amazed.]* But these were children and the memories of children.

Bishop Noonan: Children do lie. And not infrequently.

Mohammed: *[Even more amazed.]* That's your defence? You're going to stand before the face of God and tell her that children lie?

Bishop Noonan: You're twisting my words. *[Sitting back down, Bishop Noonan adopts a posture of defeat. Pausing, then speaking to no one in particular.]* They just don't get it! They can question me, berate me, for another month, another year – it will still be the same. I didn't know; we didn't know. The Vatican cautioned us in our dealings with the authorities. We did our own internal investigations and we felt that many priests were being unjustly accused. The priests had rights as well. You just didn't run to the police because some ten year old said father had touched him. We hold the priesthood in high regard; it is not to be maligned. You simply don't fire a priest as you do the secretary who's watching pornography on her computer. It's not the same. *[Exhausted.]* I am done. I have nothing further to say!

[On the patio outside the café, Gabriella is sitting at a table with her eyes closed. She appears to be meditating. AJ stumbles into the patio. He too looks like a disaster: hair and beard showing the same two months of growth; his t-shirt and sweat pants are noticeably dirty. He begins to retch – goes through a series of dry heaves. AJ sees Gabriella and heads towards her. He is upset, not angry, but sickened by his experience.]

AJ: How long was I in there?

Gabriella: In earth time? Let's see 15,000 victims at maybe five minutes each, plus your wives, girlfriends and colleagues and a few other miscellaneous screw-ups – about 70 days.

AJ: Not fun.

Gabriella: No, definitely not. Yours was one of the more difficult examinations.

AJ: One would think that after the first one hundred deaths that you would be inured to the suffering, but you are not. Every death I watched was if it was the one and only. The emotional disgust never let up, although some were more painful than others. The children were the worst; and babies...

I thought it would be like a movie, but there was no editing. And all the comments before the killing and all the comments after – the sick jokes and depraved indifference were all there for me to see and hear. We not only killed these people, we destroyed the souls of the soldiers. No wonder they kill themselves when they go home.

Upon reflection, it was easy to hold court at dinner parties and pontificate about starting a war and how we can't let this dictator get away with killing his own people, except we've never found a way to do that without us killing the very same people. And then we assign different identities to this group of civilians. The ones that he kills are real people and his killings are murder and crimes against humanity. The ones we kill are not even human – simply an adjective and a noun. Collateral damage.

Gabriella: Surely this idea gave you pause when you discussed this war.

AJ: Discussion is just words. Oh, it can be heated and passionate and often fueled by wine and false praise; and, it's very pleasing to win an argument while ridiculing your opponents, but the media and the politicians and the essayists and the pundits rarely have any skin in the game. Our daughters and sons are not going to die. For this war, those of us who stayed home got tax cuts while we let the soldiers do our killing. *[AJ sits down beside Gabriella. Speaking much softer now.]* Explain something for me. Many of the people from my personal life who spoke with me are still alive. How is it possible that they could be seen to be holding me personally accountable?

Gabriella: Sin has an energy of its own, whether it be directed at God or any part of creation. In the same manner as realistic images interact with you when you dream, here this transgression energy shapes the images and the conversations, which are projected on your mind.

AJ: So they weren't real?

Gabriella: Are not dreams real, hopes, aspirations? What about those mathematical equations that formulate in your mind? Are they not real? Perhaps you mean tangible? Could you hold it, confine it in a box? In that sense nothing here is tangible. Heaven and hell are the realms of the spirit. Your existence has not ended; it has been transformed.

AJ: *[Long pause, while reflecting on what next.]* Boy, was I an asshole!

I thought that the personal stuff would be the hardest and don't get me wrong, it was hard. You just don't realize what words and actions – which seem so trivial at the time – can do to another person. A simple act of infidelity – is never a simple act – but a major betrayal. These acts caused months of anguish for my wife (my wives). I suppose I knew that on some academic level, but never thought about it emotionally. It's the realization that this kind of personal sin had the same impact as striking her with a knife or punching her in the face – which are things I would never have done. Worse yet, I would have judged another as being a savage for having done so. I was civilized, special, a member of the elite. We would never resort to violence. And yet we violated each other emotionally and mentally – with the same results.

But, the challenge of my support for the war – that was shattering. You had tried to prepare me with your notes and Maggie warned me, but I dismissed both of your efforts. You know, in fact, I was quite excited about the idea of defending my position on the war. I assumed that I would be challenged intellectually by a most worthy opponent. I was prepared; I could hardly wait for the debate to begin. What was it Maggie said – prepare for "an argument of severe simplicity." I was not ready for a young mother and her children. How do you answer a ten year old who asks why America thought it was good to kill her family?

The Lobby Café, 3rd Visit

I couldn't answer. On reflection, I did, but it was well before the fact. I got sucked into the whole patriotic war fever. It was so ego boosting. When I penned that article in *The New Yorker* in support of the war, I was greeted like a conquering hero by the powers on the right. Here was the eloquent die-hard leftist crossing to the other side. They cultivated me with praise and thanks for having the courage to state the obvious – Saddam was pure evil – and we were fully justified in regime change in Iraq.

Switching sides was a sign of great intellectual integrity – this was the right thing to do. And I became a champion for 'our' military. We could invade with minimum loss of civilian life; that our smart bombs and targeting would be so precise that mistakes were highly unlikely; that the media would be imbedded with the troops to ensure accurate reporting. Oh, I bought the whole lie. And then the invasion with the live TV, as if we were present at the opening ceremonies of the Olympics complete with a major fireworks display. Except, these fireworks were deadly and people were dying. We were going to destroy their will to resist with the 'Shock and Awe' tactic. We would scare them into submission. But I don't recall anyone, not one reporter, ever asking who the 'they' were.

How many children under the age of twelve were living in Bagdad in March 2003? If the adults were to be frightened into submission, what was our expectation for the children? If we had no plan in place for counting civilian deaths, how were we going to respond to the mental health impact we were about to inflict on a whole generation of Iraqi children?

And not one person in the administration or the military objected, and most of those in charge had children and grandchildren of their own. But the Iraqi children were the other. We simply did not care. *[Pause; reflecting.]* If I were God, I'd send the whole lot of us to hell. We could keep Saddam company. *[Looking like he had forgot something. AJ stands; then Gabriella as well. They walk slowly away from the patio while conversing.]*

Oh, there was nothing in that whole ordeal about my failure to acknowledge God. I thought that might be important.

Gabriella: You get to answer to those commandments directly to her.

AJ: *[Somewhat flippantly.]* So is that next? I get to meet God, tell her I'm sorry, decide heaven or hell, and then I'm in or out depending upon my choice. And if I choose in, how soon do I get to meet Einstein? I'm not really intrigued about meeting God, but the chance of meeting Einstein…

Gabriella: Not quite.

AJ: Why am I not surprised that there are a few wrinkles yet in this process? You know, Gabriella, I'm not one hundred percent convinced as yet. As horrible as that examination of conscience was, this could still be one long nightmare. As for the reading–out-loud gimmick – I've only your word as proof that those who dream can't do that. And if you're part of the dream, the argument becomes circular and is worthless. Thus far, I've seen no real evidence that God actually exists. *[Gabriella simply looks at AJ.]* What, nothing to say?

Gabriella: It's not my role to persuade you.

AJ: OK, I get that. But what can I expect? Surely you can tell me something – and please no crib notes nor meetings with wives or children.

Gabriella: You have a one-on-one with God. And I can't prep you as no one knows her mind. Everyone's experience with her is truly unique. And she will let you know your requirements. I do know and can tell you two things. First, you can't nuance your way into heaven – a complete act of contrition for all your sins cannot be faked. Second, if you have a true conversion experience, do not expect an immediate entrance into heaven – that only happens for children. Everyone else, including the most saintly among you, must be prepared to experience a period of self-imposed exile – purgatory, if you wish – to cleanse the soul of all stain of sin. Only pure souls reside with God!

AJ: Again, the twist. This is like buying a time-share. Just when you think you're ready to sign the contract, there's another condition.

I appreciate the effort you've made to help me get to heaven; and, although I could have done without the examination experience, I'm ready to simply pass on this next step. What happens if I choose not to meet with her?

Gabriella: Sorry, not an option. Everyone gets a meeting.

AJ: So be it.

[Back inside the café Bishop Noonan and Mohammed are still sitting at the table.]

Bishop Noonan: Can you help me?

Mohammed: Bishop, what do you need?

Bishop Noonan: Do you know what they want from me? Those witnesses? God herself?

Mohammed: I have a pretty good idea.

Bishop Noonan: Then please share it with me. I'm lost here.

Mohammed: It's not complicated. They want you to acknowledge that your acts of omission were criminal and seriously sinful.

Bishop Noonan: What?

The Lobby Café, 3rd Visit

Mohammed: They want you to stand before the face of God and say so. Frankly, they are all tired of the "We didn't know…" They view that as a weak and pathetic attempt to evade responsibility.

Bishop Noonan: *[Self-righteously.]* I have examined my conscience a thousand times and I do not believe that what I did was a grave sin. I did my best; we simply did not know.

Mohammed: You need to stop feeling sorry for yourself. Compared to the victims, you have it easy.

Bishop Noonan: How dare you. I'm not feeling sorry for myself and I refuse to take responsibility for things beyond my control. And you must be mad to think that this has been easy on me.

Mohammed: All you need to do is set aside your pride and admit to being wrong. Those children and their parents have to overcome a visceral hatred for you and your priests. In order to pass through these doors, they have to forgive you!

11
The Holy of Holies

The Holy of Holies rests within a geodesic dome, one hundred and fifty feet in diameter. The entire inside surfaces are covered in projection screens. On the floor in the centre is a raised platform, three feet in height and forty feet square. On the side facing the doors, there is a set of stairs running the full length of the square. The other three sides fall off directly to the floor. Centred on the elevated platform is a carpet, twenty feet square. Four sanctuary lamps – from simple to elaborate – are suspended from the ceiling at various heights above the carpet. Various vessels for the burning of incense – thurible, smudge bowl, incense stands – are located around three sides of the carpet. Incense is visibly rising from the vessels. Adjacent to the stairs is a single prie-dieu with an accompanying chair and a valet stand on which is draped a prayer shawl – white with blue stripes. Beside the doors is another valet stand on which are draped two robes and a cincture. Beside the stand is a shoe mat.

As Gabriella and AJ enter the dome, the screens are resplendent with images of the universe – stars, galaxies, nebulae, planets. Gabriella is dressed entirely in white and wearing her sandals. AJ is wearing his t-shirt and sweat pants (freshly laundered) and his flip-flops. He is clean shaven, and his hair has been cut.

All in silence, Gabriella stops and removes her sandals, and places them on the mat. She looks at AJ, and he does likewise. She moves to the valet stand, removes a beige coloured robe, and gives it to AJ to put on. It is ankle length with wide sleeves and does up in the front. Gabriella then dons the other robe – a white hooded monk's robe, also ankle length. She then takes the cincture – gold – and ties it around her waist. Gabriella takes AJ by the hand, and leads him to the prie-dieu, where she motions for him to kneel. The screens go dark.

AJ: *[Still looking at the screens, he is unable to recognize an obvious sacred space.]* Kneeling? I don't do kneeling. Do I really need to wear this outfit? What's with going barefoot?

Gabriella: *[Sternly.]* You would be wise to adopt an attitude of reverence and not trifle with things beyond your grasp. If that's not possible, then simply be respectful of me in my prayers, and be silent. *[Gabriella removes the prayer shawl from the second valet stand…]* Baruch atah Adonai. Eloheinu melech ha olam. *[…and places it around her shoulders.]*

[Gabriella climbs the stairs, moves to the edge of the carpet and then pulls the hood of her robe up to cover her head. The sanctuary lights begin to burn. Gabriella steps onto the carpet and she starts to glow from the inside – low at first and then brighter as she approaches the centre. She takes on a more ethereal appearance, more spirit-like.] Here I am Lord. I come to do your will.

AJ: *[AJ jumps up from the kneeler.]* Whoa…Gabriella, what's happening to you?

Gabriella: We are now beyond the physical limitations of the Lobby and are moving into the realm of the spirit. You are now seeing me as I really am. *[Gabriella kneels on the carpet, and then prostrates herself with her face buried in her folded arms. Gabriella remains in this position for several minutes. She then stands, turns around, and approaches AJ.]* AJ, I'm going to take my leave from you now. You are to remain here. I will see you when you are finished. May God have mercy on you.

[Gabriella gives AJ a hug, and kisses him on both cheeks. She then leaves the dome. She is still glowing.]

AJ: *[AJ looks around. He sits in the chair; looks around some more. He stands up, and climbs the stairs. He walks around the carpet checking out the incense, but is very careful not to step on the carpet. He speaks flippantly.]* Well, I'm here.

    I'm waiting…

I'm waiting...

I'm waiting for the show – the proof of your existence. What's it going to be? The thunder, the lightning, perhaps a choir of heavenly hosts singing the Halleluiah Chorus. Or maybe the scare tactics: an earthquake or scenes of tormented souls in hell, right out of Dante. What's it going to be? I know, my mother will appear in a cloud and call me by my childhood nick-name. Then I'll turn into mush.

[Silence. Then the sanctuary lamps flare and there is a light wind, evident in the movement of the smoke from the incense. AJ feels the wind and shudders and wraps his arms around himself.]

God: *[A distinctive female voice, soft.]* "Be still, and know that I am God!"[9]

AJ: *[AJ turns this way and that. He looks apprehensive. Then it starts: mathematical equations are projected on the surfaces of the dome, starting with Newton's work, then Einstein's, Hawking's, and others. AJ looks and then starts to pay very close attention. Equations speed up.]* You have my attention. *[Equations speed up.]* Wait, wait, slow down! Some of this is new. *[Equations slowdown.]* OK, very good. No, wait, go back please. *[Equations back up. Then progress again.]* Wow, this is all new to me. I see it. I see where this leads. Please stop, hold it there! This is way beyond me. Is there more? *[Equations continue for several more minutes. Then the screens go dark.]*

For the first time in my life, I feel ignorant. I feel small, like I'm standing in the presence of greatness. But what kind of greatness are you? This doesn't prove that you are God, only someone smarter than me.

God: Let your own words be the judge.

[A video now appears on the surfaces of the dome. In a large auditorium, a debate is set to begin between two teams of three people. A large sign reads, "Ultimate Debates". Tonight: God is an Illusion! AJ is at the podium, and begins to speak. "Our opponents – supposedly worthy, although I wouldn't apply that adjective – have doctoral degrees in theology from prestigious universities. A question should be posed: what value is a doctoral degree in theology? There is no God, thus the study of God is a fraud. Worse, a joke. Theology is a field of made up knowledge. What famous educational institutions offer degrees in Tarot Card Reading or Astrology? As Freud said, "god is an illusion." Imagine spending a lifetime creating an entire body of knowledge about your imaginary friend. That's theology!

Now in fairness, there is value in the study of their 'sacred texts', but only as literature or commentaries on history. There was validity in the study of the gods before the advance of science when humankind did not understand the physics and mathematics of the universe. But certainly no longer.

Our team, in contrast, is comprised of three of the most brilliant scientific minds who have spent our lifetimes studying the physical universe – not illusions, not fairy tales. In fact, any being smarter than me and my colleagues would have to be your fictitious god." The last sentence is written across the bottom of the video. AJ applauds silently.]

AJ: Well played! Supposing you are God? What do you want from me? Or rather, what's the price of residency in your heaven, and more critically, access to that knowledge? *[AJ looks reflectively towards the sanctuary lamps; he is listening to a silent voice, nodding.]* That's the entry requirements: Love you and your children. I must admit that after your display of knowledge, love for you would seem to be very doable. But love your children? To paraphrase the famous biblical question: who are your children?

God: These are all my children. *[A series of slides come up on the surfaces of the dome. Collages of people and groups of people: children, women, men, families, disabled, able-bodied, diverse, young and old, the good and the bad and the terrible (the terrible include Stalin, Hitler, Pol Pot, Saddam, Assad, etc.). The last few slides include AJ, his parents, his wives, his children and his lovers.]*

AJ: I must say I'm getting more impressed by the minute. You didn't miss anyone in my life and my liaisons with several of those young women were only known to me – and them. But some of your children were and are the most heinous of human beings. How could I love them? How could you love them?

God: There is nothing that I have created that I do not love. The fact that some of my creatures do not love me in return, and have chosen to live in eternity beyond my presence, grieves me. But I gave each of them a choice. The same choice that I give to you.

[AJ stands fixated on the sanctuary lights. He now realizes that the time has come for a decision. As the sanctuary lights get brighter, the entire dome begins to shimmer with an increasingly white brilliance. AJ tries to protect his eyes as he sinks to his knees, looking heavenward.]

12
The Lobby Café, 4th Visit

Outside the café Gabriella, no longer wearing the white robe, is sitting at a table. AJ approaches, sees Gabriella and rushes over to her. AJ is in his usual clothes with the robe draped over his arm. He quickly tosses the robe over a chair. He is quite excited.

AJ: I have so much to tell you! My mind is running faster than my mouth. How can I explain it – surely you know. Of course you know, you were there at the end. Oh, I've got to tell Paul. Have you seen him?

Gabriella: He's inside talking with Mohammed. *[AJ makes a move to go inside.]* I don't think we should interrupt at this moment.

AJ: OK. Where was I?…yes, you were there…but before I get to that part did you know she showed me the answer to the theory of everything. She showed me the mathematical foundations of Einstein's theory of relativity and the mathematics of quantum mechanics and – this was astounding –

the equations that link the two together. She began with basic formulae from Newton and Planck, then on to work by Heisenberg, Higgs and Hawking, and finally she moved way beyond me. Yet, it wasn't a ruse. When I asked her to slow it down or go back, she did. She waited for me to process it. And when it became too profound, I asked if there was more – and there was much more. I'm only theorizing, but it very much looked like equations that dealt with the ideas of parallel universes, dark matter, dark energy and who knows what else. It was like being immersed in a pool of pure brilliance. *[Still talking quickly, as if trying to get it all out before he forgets.]*

Then there were these pictures, collages of people – the good and the bad, the ugly and the beautiful – children, women, men, families, famous and infamous, common folk, all sizes, colours and abilities; and then she told me that all of these were her children and that she loved them all equally. And there appeared to be a sadness to her – it was a feeling that I had, which came upon me quite suddenly, a sadness that many of her children had chosen not to love her in return. I told her that this idea – to love all was beyond human comprehension and ability.

And then I was simply infused with the knowledge that I would soon need to decide where I would spend my eternity. And if being with God was where I was leaning, then three things would be required: love, first and foremost, of God and all her creatures and…

Gabriella: So do you think you could love that way?

AJ: No, not really. But I sense that it is a requirement and I do see her point. Further, the love she is talking about is not the love that human's most often reference. It's all about wanting the very best for the other – always and without consideration of the self.

Gabriella: Well done! And the other two conditions?

AJ: In all honesty, these are easier than the first. The acknowledgment of all my earthly transgressions. I now realize what a screw-up I was, so saying so doesn't seem so onerous; and, as to the self-imposed exile to heal my soul – I think if you are able to comply with the first and second conditions – then you would welcome number three. Because it gets you to her!

Gabriella: *[Nodding and smiling.]* You are almost there!

AJ: *[Realizing that he has been sidelined in his story.]* Can I finish my account? Now where was I? Oh yes, there was this long pause and I didn't know whether I was supposed to speak or not or if the meeting was over. And let me tell you, I thought if this is it, then I'm not overly impressed. I got the math part and the love idea – if true – is beyond comprehension, but I was looking for a knock-down revelation. And that had not happened. And then it did. Just like that! *[AJ seems lost in his recollection. Says nothing more.]*

Gabriella: Yes? You were saying.

AJ: *[Trying to get the recollection right.]* The lights – you know the hanging lights... *[AJ can't find the word.]*

Gabriella: The sanctuary lamps?

AJ: Yes, yes, those lights. They started to increase in intensity, not in size but brilliance and I felt a corresponding energy pulse throughout my body. There was a trilling from head to toe that grew proportionally to the growth of the lamps. And I knew then that I was about to see God as she truly is. *[AJ now sits down at the table and speaks directly to Gabriella.]*

I was expecting big and powerful, but that's not what happened. Suddenly, I was looking down on a vast plain and the day was perfect, bright and warm. And I realized that I had the power to zoom in and out – like Google Earth – and I noted that the plain was not smooth but covered in small mounds, and the trees that outlined the perimeter were completely defoliated and charred. So I zoomed in and to my horror the entire plain was covered in human remains – women and men – soldiers with their armaments and camp followers from every epoch of human history. There were swords and bucklers, shields and long-bows, body armour and firearms, from muskets to rifles and machine guns. And the bodies – were endless. And despite the terrible stench that filled the air, the bodies seemed fresh in their death with blood still oozing from wounds and dismembered limbs. I was repulsed and gagged to the point of vomiting, but I could not look away.

Then I saw two figures moving about the bodies, not so much as walking but floating mere millimeters above everything. I zoomed in to see what they were doing and I recognized you, Gabriella, and you were accompanying the other being and supporting her under one arm. And this person turned and looked in my direction; and, although I saw her clearly, I cannot describe any details of her face except to say it was a combination of inconsolable grief and love – the way I expect that a mother must feel when holding a dying child. And this person was bending down to touch the face of each body as if anointing it. And then I heard it: a very faint wail that emanated from this person – and I realized that this was God and she was weeping for her children. I went looking for power and strength, and what I found was love and tears. *[A] abruptly stands up, goes quickly to the door and opens it.]* I've got to tell Paul.

Gabriella: Wait, wait... *[Gabriella states softly as AJ disappears through the doors.]* I'm not sure that's a good idea...

[AJ enters the café enthusiastically, leaving Gabriella alone on the patio. Bishop Noonan is sitting by himself. He is dressed in his cassock, which has been cleaned and pressed. His hair has been cut, and he is clean shaven. A beige robe is draped over an empty chair.]

AJ: *[AJ starts in without looking at Bishop Noonan's demeanour.]* Paul, Paul...let me begin by asking for your forgiveness. I truly have been an asshole. Sorry, and...

Bishop Noonan: *[Sarcastically.]* Well listen to you. All full of love are we? She must have made quite the impression? What did she do? Mesmerize you with some feats of knowledge? Show you some flashes of lightning? Something seems to have excited you. No? Yes?

AJ: *[Somewhat confused.]* Yes...yes...yes...she did all of that. Well no, I don't remember any lightning. But the feats of knowledge part, she did do that. She revealed to me the answer to the idea of the unified theory. For one brief moment I knew how the universe operated and I felt the tremendous power of the force that holds it all together – the heart of God that beats throughout the whole of creation. It was a powerful moment, a syncretisation of knowledge and emotion. I actually cried; and I haven't cried since I...

Bishop Noonan: I'm jealous. I think I missed the entire experience. I can't get past my anger. I gave her everything – my life, my daily prayer and worship, my devotion. I was the faithful priest who served my parishes well; I worked six and seven day weeks; I rarely took vacations; I was always there; I never questioned the faith; I was the loyal servant; I…I…I…and yet I'm being held accountable for the action of others. I keep telling people…I told her…we just didn't know. The times were very different in those days.

AJ: *[AJ now understands Bishop Noonan is severely conflicted over his experience with his God.]* What are you going to do?

Bishop Noonan: *[Ignoring the question, Bishop Noonan continues to talk.]* And look at you all gushy over God, and until this moment you didn't even acknowledge her presence. Did you ever say thank you for your own existence and the gifts you so undeservedly received? No, you chalked everything up to happenchance: born into a wealthy family in the twentieth century in the USA; smart genes; white; good looking; healthy. You had everything going for you and never once did you say 'thank you'. In fact, you laughed at the idea of God and ridiculed her adherents. And now you're all bubble-

gummy about her 'Oh Wow'! Furthermore, you get a chance at heaven, the same as me...and let's look at the prayer score: thousands of hours – me; you – zero! How is that right? Can you rationalize that? *[Bishop Noonan pauses, shakes his head.]*
  What was your question?

AJ: What are you going to do?

Bishop Noonan: I don't know. I really don't know. How absurd is that? I've spent my whole adult life preparing for today and now that it's arrived, I'm not sure what I'm going to do. *[Not really interested.]* So what about you?

AJ: What's to choose? To live forever in the presence of pure knowledge and pure love; or not. But what's more surprising is this peace I have about her requirement that all who seek her presence be purified – this self-imposed exile. It is the answer to your question. Why do I even get this chance? It's her way of giving her wayward children one last opportunity to come home. It is the ultimate prodigal child story. *[Stating definitively, surprising himself.]* So I have decided that forty-two years in exile would be appropriate.

Bishop Noonan: What?

AJ: One day for each of the 15,000 Iraqis that I met in my examination of conscience, plus an extra year to atone for the multitude of hurts directed at my family, friends, colleagues, and students. One day for every person: to learn their names and their personal histories and to write a letter of heartfelt apology to each for my transgressions. A letter to be personally delivered at the cessation of my time of atonement.

Bishop Noonan: What about meeting with Einstein?

AJ: He will be there when I arrive.

Bishop Noonan: That's your answer. You're now prepared to wait for forty-two years for a meeting that couldn't wait? You're infuriating. You come here with no preparation, not a word of acceptance of God's presence anywhere and now you are at complete peace and willing to spend half a human lifetime in purgatory in remission of sins that you never recognized as having committed. *[With emphasis.]* You do realize that once you enter this period of exile that you are guaranteed entrance to heaven. Although delayed, you are saved. And then there's me – a lifetime of commitment to God and I'm completely lost. Do you comprehend the injustice in this? I should be in your shoes and you should be going straight to hell.

AJ: *[Countering.]* I may have been a non-believer, but I was never ignorant of what 'religious people' practiced. Was it not part of your obligations to pray for people – for people precisely like me? I wasn't the only heathen on earth. Did you not have family and friends who rejected God; and did you not pray for them? Unless I miss-heard the prayers at your weddings and funerals, you continued to pray for them even after death. So were those prayers empty words? Were you simply going through the motions? Did you not expect those prayers to be heard? Perhaps someone – even you – prayed for me and now those prayers have been answered!

Bishop Noonan: *[Sarcastically.]* Well look who wants to be my spiritual director. If that's what happened, then you better thank someone else because I never prayed for you.

AJ: Wow, you are angry!

Bishop Noonan: "If today you hear her voice, harden not your hearts."[10]

AJ: I'm sorry, what's that?

Bishop Noonan: 95th Psalm. I'm afraid that the light of God cannot penetrate a heart so unwilling to let it in. I'm so…so…annoyed at her that I've shut her out completely. *[They stare at each other, knowing that all meaningful discussion between them is over.]* So what do you think happens next?

AJ: I think you just choose. I think you just decide to ask for forgiveness, take ownership of all your transgressions and pledge your profound regret. I think I need to pray. *[Pausing.]* I can't believe that I, Dr. AJ Forsythe, just said that! *[Thinking.]*

Dear God: Is that how you start? *[Noticing that Bishop Noonan is not paying attention to him, AJ adopts a reflective pose and continues.]*

For all the times I looked at the stars and failed to see your hand, I am sorry.

For all the times I treated your children as subjects of my ridicule, I am sorry.

For all the times I objectified women for my own personal gratification, I am sorry.

For all the times I failed to make your earth a better place, I am sorry.

For being far less a man than I could have been, I am sorry.

[As AJ makes his act of contrition, Gabriella approaches him from behind. She is carrying a purple stole across one arm.]

Bishop Noonan: Someone is here for you.

AJ: Pardon? *[Bishop Noonan points to behind AJ. AJ turns and sees Gabriella.]*

Gabriella: Alex, it is time! *[AJ instinctively understands what is happening. He stands and moves towards Gabriella.]*

Gabriella: Bow you head and receive God's blessing. *[AJ bows his head and Gabriella places the stole about AJ's shoulders and proclaims.]* Today there is great joy in heaven.

[An alleluia chorus[11] begins. AJ and Gabriella leave the café together as the chorus continues.]

[The chorus ends and Bishop Noonan sits alone in silence. He pushes back from the table, stands and leaves the café. Outside, he looks up and speaks directly to God.]

Bishop Noonan: No more witnesses. No Mohammed. No Gabriella. No Alex. It's just you and me. In my mind I know what you want from me, but I'm not sure that I can give it. You want me to take this cross entirely upon my shoulders, to fully accept the blame for the abuse scandal in my diocese. You want me to be the fall guy for your errant priests – for this flawed church. You want me to lie prostrate before you and empty myself of all pride and admit freely to this guilt. You want me to acknowledge that my activities only made the scandal worse; that the children were more important than the diocese, the Holy See, than all else…that I should have had the courage to resign…that the church was desperate for a leader who would have risked everything to tell the truth about the abuse. You wanted someone who would challenge the hierarchy all the way to Rome, regardless of any consequences. You needed a saint and no one stepped forward. Well, I certainly wasn't that guy. It never occurred to me to be that guy. I and the other bishops simply did the human thing – we circled the wagons and hoped the issue would go away.

You think I don't understand. I do. You think that I made the Holy Roman Catholic Church my

God. And now, you want me to accept – no rejoice would be your verb, yes rejoice – that that philanderer... *[pointing to where AJ was]*...has recanted and is now worthy of heaven. That he has reached an equivalency with me! You want me to acknowledge your generosity without being jealous.

I know what you want. But I want something too. I want you to acknowledge that I was a good and faithful servant; that I did my best; that I deserve a place in your kingdom. I want you to be grateful! I resent the fact that after everything I have done for you, I'm having to beg for a place at your side, while that...that... whatever, has now been welcomed with open arms. I deserve better. And if you can't be forthcoming, then I don't think I want to be with you.

I don't think I can do it. I can't! I won't.

13
The Party

There's a party in full flight! The setting is a high-ceilinged ballroom decorated with balloons and banners in bright colours. High cocktail tables, replete with an assortment of hors d'oeuvres, are distributed about the room. Entrance to the room is by way of a curved stairway from an upper balcony. At the top of the stairs a Doorwoman is checking invitations and announcing the arrival of the guests. Music is playing (Led Zeppelin, Stairway to Heaven). Waitresses adorned in simple black dresses are serving drinks. The guests are all former members of faith communities, and are all dressed in appropriate garb. They include: A pope in whites; a Russian Orthodox bishop in full vestments; an Anglican bishop in full vestments; nuns in habits and robes – Christian, Hindu, Buddhist and Shinto; women and men in Roman collars or choir robes; monks in robes – Hindu, Buddhist and Christian; a Zoroastrian priest; a Muslim imam; a Muslim woman in a burka; an Hasidic Jewish male in black hat and coat; a Jewish male wearing a tallit, kippah and tefillin; shamans and priests from ancient and indigenous religions; a Shinto priest; a Sikh guru; an old world Mennonite couple; women in extremely conservative dress — long skirts, full sleeves, covered heads. Also a solitary Young Woman, standing on her own. She is dressed in a black suit with matching shirt and tie.

Bishop Noonan arrives. He is dressed in Choir Dress with a Cappa Magna. Everyone, except Bishop Noonan, is wearing aviator mirrored sunglasses.

Doorwoman: Ladies and Gentlemen, may I present his Excellency, Bishop Paul Noonan. *[Everyone turns to face the stairs. Loud applause. Bishop Noonan descends the stairs and is met by Dimitri, the host of the party.]*

Dimitri: *[Dimitri is the Russian Orthodox bishop. He has an Eastern European accent. He greets Bishop Noonan with a big hug and cheek kisses.]* Noonan – we've heard that you might be joining us...welcome! With your addition we have enough for a synod ...ha...ha! *[Dimitri introduces Bishop Noonan to other guests. Waves to a waitress.]* Amanda, bring the bishop a scotch.

Bishop Noonan: Oh, no, no...

Dimitri: Noonan, remember where you are. This is the place for indulging. There's no Lenten fast down here.

Bishop Noonan: Oh, yes. Yes, a drink would be great.

Dimitri: It does take some time to get accustomed to this lifestyle, especially for us clerical types – no prayers, no fasting, and no duties at all. So tell me, how was your experience with her – isn't she something? All that power and all that beauty, but zero appreciation of everything we've done – and on her behalf no less. Was that your experience?

Bishop Noonan: You as well? Yes, not one bit of thanks. Only, "You should have done better."

Dimitri: Ingrate! *[Dimitri continues talking, but is now obviously bored with Bishop Noonan. He keeps looking beyond Bishop Noonan at other party guests while he makes small talk. It is apparent to Bishop Noonan that Dimitri is no longer focused on him. Bishop Noonan starts to look around as well. Amanda, the waitress, approaches with Bishop Noonan's drink. She is a big-breasted woman.]*

Amanda: Excellency, your scotch. *[Bishop Noonan takes the drink and stares obviously at her breasts.]*

Dimitri: That's it Noonan, have a good long look. Very impressive, wouldn't you say? She might even give you a feel! Ha, ha…first time for everything. *[Bishop Noonan looks a little embarrassed.]* What? What else can happen to you? No confessional here!

Bishop Noonan: Oh, right. Haven't quite adjusted.

[The party continues with the guests mingling about, shaking hands with the new guy. Bishop Noonan finishes off his drink, partakes of some food, and then has another drink

as he circulates. The guests slowly drift away save for Bishop Noonan, Amanda and the Young Woman.]

Young Woman: You may go, Amanda, we're done for tonight. *[The Young Woman approaches Bishop Noonan.]* Excellency, I'm so pleased to see you here. I wasn't at all sure that I would get you. But here you are!

Bishop Noonan: And you are?

Young Woman: I am known by many names. For you, my name is Pride!

Bishop Noonan: I think I'm missing something.

Young Woman: I've been your own personal demon for many years. Each night I would visit you and whisper in your ear, "You are a great bishop; you are doing a great job; you need to protect the church from these vicious lies; you need to protect the priesthood, the most noble of all callings."

Bishop Noonan: *[Bishop Noonan is having trouble processing this statement, so he switches topics.]* I see. Tell me, did you have the same choice as me? I mean between her and here? Are you happy here?

Young Woman: We are elated when we get someone of your calibre to join us. When we win, she loses! *[Somewhat reflectively.]* We were 'happy' once – when it was just her and us. You humans ruined our paradise.

Bishop Noonan: And now the enticement of humans drives your existence?

Young Woman: Don't you just love irony!

Bishop Noonan: You say you are a demon – how long have you been here?

Young Woman: I'm one of the originals. I've been here since the fall. We tried to convince her, but she was adamant. We all watched the evolution of your species. You have to give her credit – her physical creation was simply spectacular. But then she said that these creatures – humans – should become like us, her spiritual beings. She was going to infuse these beings with a soul, and thus grant them immortality. Then they could be with us after their earthly demise.

That pronouncement was not well received. She did listen to our argument, but in the end she elected to move forward with her decision. I remember it very clearly when she informed us, "I have heard your concerns, but these creatures – humans as we have called them – are worthy of the opportunity to be one with us." That statement triggered the great revolt. Lucifer – a magnificent archangel, even more beautiful than Gabriella – stood before her and said, "This is a monumental error! Shall I, who am light and flame share heaven with mud and dust?"[12] At first it was just the two of them, then many angels joined with Lucifer and there was a great clamoring of voices expressing opposition to her decision.

She never raised her voice; she simply said, "My decision has been made. You can disagree, but there will be no rebellion. You have free will and thus you have a choice: stay in my presence or leave. I offer no persuasion. You must decide on your own." Then she paused to ensure that she had our complete attention. "Be aware that if you choose to leave, my grace will no longer be your constant companion. You will live in darkness for eternity." Then Lucifer said, "We cannot accept these creatures as ever being worthy of sharing heaven with us. If it is your will to proceed as you have stated, then I and my followers" – there was a great gasp at the use of this word, as there had never been factions in heaven – "will leave together. Believe me when I say that we will prove to you their unworthiness."

She said to all of us, "Reflect wisely and make your choice – Lucifer or me, knowing that your decision can never be undone." And many of us chose Lucifer. And in an instant we were gone from her presence. So, yes, I too had the same choice as you.

Bishop Noonan: So was it the right decision?
Young Woman: Depends. Our whole existence revolves around vengeance and proving that she was and continues to be wrong about humankind.

And you, Excellency, are our latest trophy. If you thrive on hate, then this is the place to be!

Bishop Noonan: *[Once again Bishop Noonan is having trouble processing, so he switches topics.]* So what's with the sunglasses?

Young Woman: You'll find that no one here really cares about what you have to say, so these allow us to keep up the impression that we're paying attention by hiding our eyes behind the mirrors. *[Hands Bishop Noonan a pair of mirrored aviator sunglasses.]* Bishop, here's your very own pair. Try them on. *[Bishop Noonan puts on the sunglasses.]* Looks great. I can't tell what you are looking at, or even if your eyes are open. You can now be as phony as the rest of us.

Bishop Noonan: *[Looks around the room, testing out the glasses.]* This wasn't what I was expecting – actually, I wasn't expecting to be here at all. *[Trying to put on a happy face.]* Well today wasn't so bad – in fact it was very good. The company was very impressive; the scotch was good – no great, best I have ever had; the food was terrific; and now that I can look, the women were spectacular, especially that Amanda.

Young Woman: Be advised Bishop, here things are not all they appear to be. The scotch, though great, does not impair. The food, also great, never satisfies. And Amanda, well you can lust all you want, but you will never experience her.

Bishop Noonan: Is there anything to look forward to? *[Darkness starts to settle in.]*

Young Woman: Yes, of course. Tomorrow and every day, we'll have another party as we await our new arrivals. It's the one period of excitement we get to experience every day. We never know who will choose to be with us!

Bishop Noonan: *[Bishop Noonan realizes that he can barely see his hands, looks about.]* It's getting dark. What do I do now?

Young Woman: Endure.

Bishop Noonan: Endure?

Young Woman: Here we still experience daytime and nighttime. The darkness we simply endure until sunrise.

Bishop Noonan: Surely I need a place to stay, a bed, some sleep?

Young Woman: No, those are physical needs. We need none of that. You will simply endure the darkness and learn to do as we do. Replenish our resentment. *[The Young Woman pauses in the last bit of twilight and Bishop Noonan stares directly at her.]* "...the heirs of the kingdom will be thrown into the outer darkness where there will be weeping and gnashing of teeth."[13]

[The Young Woman fades out completely. There is enough light to make out that Bishop Noonan is still there. There is a mournful cry and the sound of grinding teeth.]

Bishop Noonan: *[Long pause. Bishop Noonan realizes what a mistake he has made.]* Oh fuck!

Acknowledgments

Save for the support of friends, this manuscript would be ageing in an old file box. So thanks to Jack O'Brien, Mary Craig and Father Mike King for volunteering to read my first draft. Then thanks to Enzo Fazio, Jack (same guy) and Elaine O'Brien, Marlene Castura and my wife, Dawn, for workshopping the script and suggesting needed revisions. Also, thank you to Zenon Skrzypczyk, Dermot Nolan and Bob Fierheller, who provided unbiased encouragement to keep the project alive; and, to Matthew Bin for helping me navigate the realm of self-publishing.

Lastly, I am indebted to my granddaughter, Sarah, for introducing me to the world of social media, and to those Facebook friends who readily agreed to help me promote the book with their contacts.

About the Author

Peter Rosser spent 37 years in youth ministry with the Catholic Youth Organization of the Diocese of Hamilton (Ontario), the last twelve years as Executive Director.

Until this past year, when he completed this first book, *Crimes Against Children,* his professional writing had consisted of policy papers, grant applications, marketing materials and reference letters for teenagers.

Peter retired in 2007 and spent the next ten years babysitting a toddler, preparing lunch in a local soup kitchen and visiting terminally ill cancer patients.

He resides in Dundas, Ontario with his wife of 50 years, Dawn. They have two adult children and three grandchildren.

The author can be reached at peter.rosser048@gmail.com.

End Notes

1   *Johns Hopkins Bloomberg School of Public Health*, "Updated Iraq Survey Affirms Earlier Mortality Estimates," October 11, 2006.

2   Paul William Roberts, *A War Against Truth* (Vancouver: Raincoast Books, 2004), 199.

3   Albert Camus, *The Plague*, trans. Stuart Gilbert (London: Penguin Books, 2010), 127.

4   George Santayana, *Interpretations of Poetry and Religion* (Cambridge: The MIT Press, 1989), 108-109.

5   Peter Damian, *Liber Gomorrhianus*, trans. Pierre J. Payer (Waterloo: Wilfrid Laurier University Press, 1982), 61.

6   Ibid, 40.

7   Peter Rosser, "Where is the strong voice of the church?" *The Hamilton Spectator*, November 7,

2009.

8   Psalm 22:1 (The Harper Collins Study Bible Revised Edition).

9   Psalm 46:10 (The Harper Collins Study Bible Revised Edition).

10   Psalm 95:7-8, "If today you hear his voice, harden not your hearts," *Glory & Praise 2nd Edition*, ed. Randall De Bruyn (Portland: OCP Publication, 1997), #235.

11   "O Sons and Daughters," *Glory & Praise 2nd Edition*, ed. Randall De Bruyn (Portland: OCP Publication, 1997), #379.

12   Anonymous

13   Matthew 8:12 (The Harper Collins Study Bible Revised Edition).

Made in the USA
Middletown, DE
01 July 2019